The Essential
Homeschool
2nd Grade
Workbook

135 Fun Curriculum-Based Exercises to Build and Strengthen Skills in Reading, Writing, and Math

Martha Zschock

Illustrations by Collaborate Agency

ROCKRIDGE PRESS

This book belongs to:

_____

For general information on our other products and services, please contact our Customer Care Department within the United States at (866) 744-2665, or outside the United States at (510) 253-0500.

Paperback ISBN: 978-1-648-76779-1

Manufactured in the United States of America

Series Designer: Lisa Schreiber
Interior and Cover Designer: Stephanie Sumulong
Art Producer: Meg Baggott
Editor: Erum Khan
Production Editor: Sigi Nacson
Production Manager: Riley Hoffman

Illustrations © 2021 Collaborate Agency

10 9 8 7 6 5 4 3 2 1

Contents

Part 2: Writing

Language Skills

Writing Skills

Part 3: Math

Algebraic Thinking

Operations in Base Ten

Note to Homeschooling Parents

Welcome to second grade, the age of discovery! At this stage, children are developing foundational skills in reading, writing, and math, and are becoming more confident as they begin to apply those skills to the world around them. As a teacher, parent, and children's book author/illustrator, I have had the pleasure of guiding children on this exciting adventure as they become independent learners, problem solvers, and curious explorers.

Homeschooling offers parents and children the opportunity to discover the world together. What fun! Encouraging your child to make connections as they build foundational skills will help them make the leap from learning to read to reading to learn. As children begin to make connections, their worlds expand—and their excitement is contagious. Remember that you are your child's first and favorite teacher. You know your child's interests, strengths, and challenges. You are in the unique position to help them best. This can feel overwhelming, and you may question whether you are doing everything right. Take heart: this book will help supplement your child's second grade curriculum and will serve as a guide throughout the year.

The Essential Homeschool 2nd Grade Workbook is divided into three subjects: reading, writing, and math. Each subject is divided into smaller sections with color-coded tabs for quick and easy navigation. Within each section, exercises focus on specific skills aligned to common core curriculum standards. Each page highlights the skills being taught so you can easily track which standards are covered as your child works their way through the book.

As you help guide your child, remember that each child grows and develops at their own pace. What seems difficult today may be easy tomorrow. Know that you are doing a great job, and enjoy this special time together.

PART 1
Reading

1. Valuable Vowels

Vowels have two different sounds. Long vowels say their own name. Short vowels make a special sound. The **a** in **cake** makes a long vowel sound. The **a** in **cat** makes a short sound.

➡ READ each word. CIRCLE the words or pictures that have a short vowel sound. DRAW a square around the words or pictures that have a long vowel sound.

jump		pin	dress	
	fox		pet	bike
	night	cap		bug
home		see	boat	
hand	June			rain

SKILL: Long and Short Vowels

2. Listen Carefully

When a vowel sounds like its name, it is a **long vowel**. If it has a different
sound, it is a **short vowel**.

➡ READ each word. COLOR the box **red** if the word has a short vowel sound.
COLOR the box **blue** if the word has a long vowel sound. Three in a row
is tic-tac-toe!

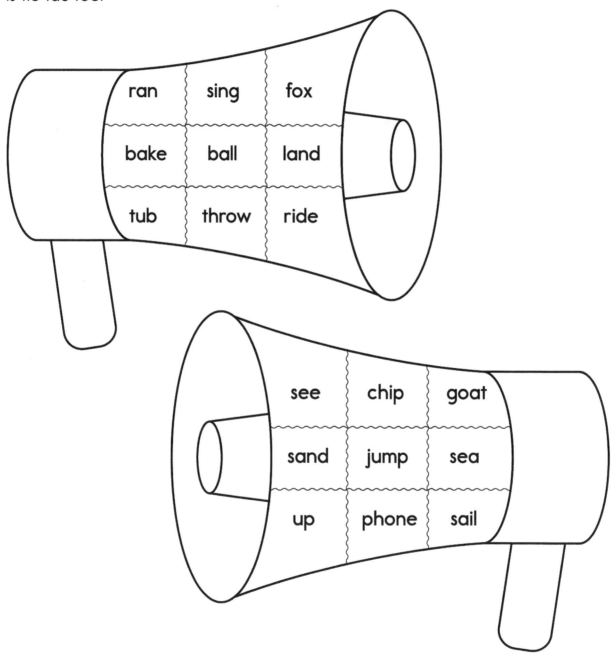

ran	sing	fox
bake	ball	land
tub	throw	ride

see	chip	goat
sand	jump	sea
up	phone	sail

SKILL: Long and Short Vowels

3. Ship Ahoy!

The letters **a**, **e**, **i**, **o**, and **u** are vowels, and sometimes **y** acts like a vowel. Vowel teams are two vowels (or **y**) joined together. The vowel teams **ai, ay, ee, ea, oa, oe, ue,** and **ui** all have the long vowel sound of the first vowel. When these two vowels join together to go "walking," the first one does the "talking"!

➡ READ each word In the picture. COLOR each section using the color in the key that matches each vowel sound. Then, color the rest of the picture.

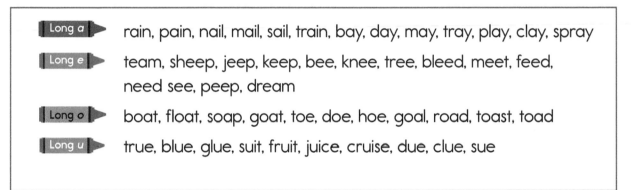

Long **a** ▶	rain, pain, nail, mail, sail, train, bay, day, may, tray, play, clay, spray
Long **e** ▶	team, sheep, jeep, keep, bee, knee, tree, bleed, meet, feed, need see, peep, dream
Long **o** ▶	boat, float, soap, goat, toe, doe, hoe, goal, road, toast, toad
Long **u** ▶	true, blue, glue, suit, fruit, juice, cruise, due, clue, sue

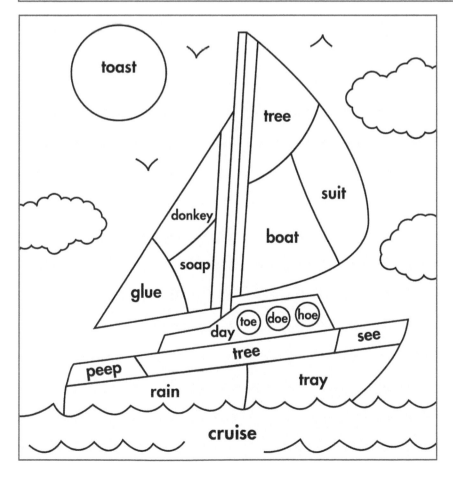

SKILL: Vowel Teams

4. Team Spirit

Two vowels that team up make one sound. Sometimes the vowel team has the long vowel sound of the first vowel. Other times the team makes its own special sound.

➡ READ each word out loud. WRITE the word in the column that matches the vowel sound you hear.

pail	day	sauce	tea	three	eight	key	pie	soon	goat
toe	voice	toy	loud	true	suit	buy	feud		

I hear a long vowel sound.	I hear a special sound.

SKILL: Vowel Teams

5. Teamwork

The vowel teams **au**, **oo**, **oi**, **ou**, and **oy** make a special sound. The first vowel sound glides into the second vowel without taking a break.

➡ READ each word in the box out loud. CIRCLE the vowel team that matches the picture. WRITE the word that matches the picture.

| coin   cloud   boil   laundry   faucet   house   moon   boy |

1. au   oy   ou

_____

2. oy   oo   au

_____

3. ou   oy   oo

_____

4. au   oo   oi

_____

5. ou   oi   oy

_____

6. oo   oy   au

_____

7. oo   oy   ou

_____

8. au   oi   oo

_____

SKILL: Vowel Teams

6. Dream Team

Becoming familiar with vowel teams will help you read and write new words. The more you practice, the easier it will get.

➡ FILL IN the missing vowel team to finish the rhyming pair of words.

1. rain — p __ __ n

2. true — bl __ __

3. cool — p __ __ l

4. coin — j __ __ n

5. play — d __ __

6. tree — b __ __

7. loud — cl __ __ d

8. eight — fr __ __ ght

9. treat — m __ __ t

10. honey — mon __ __

11. boat — fl __ __ t

12. joy — b __ __

13. suit — fr __ __ t

14. pail — s __ __ l

15. team — dr __ __ m

7. Clap to the Beat

Clap your hands as you say the word **dog**. Do you hear the beat? Now try the word **mitten**. Did you hear two beats? Words can be broken into parts called **syllables** that are like beats. Each syllable has one vowel sound.
➡ READ each word and CLAP your hands as you say each syllable. COLOR the bubble next to the choice that divides the syllables correctly.

1. **forest**
   ○ fo | rest   ○ for | est   ○ fore | st

2. **rainbow**
   ○ rain | bow   ○ rainb | ow   ○ rai | nbow

3. **garden**
   ○ ga | rden   ○ gar | den   ○ gard | en

4. **elbow**
   ○ e | lbow   ○ elb | ow   ○ el | bow

5. **turtle**
   ○ tu |rtle   ○ tur | tle   ○ turt | tle

6. **dragon**
   ○ dra | gon   ○ dr | agon   ○ drag | on

7. **cupcake**
   ○ cupc | ake   ○ cu | pcake   ○ cup | cake

8. **doctor**
   ○ do |ctor   ○ doc | tor   ○ doct | or

9. **candle**
   ○ ca | ndle   ○ cand | le   ○ can | dle

10. **basket**
    ○ bas | ket   ○ bask | et   ○ ba | sket

11. **snowman**
    ○ sno | wman   ○ snow | man   ○ snowm | an

12. **marble**
    ○ ma | rble   ○ marb | le   ○ mar | ble

SKILL: Letter Patterns

8. Harvest Time

Some words have one syllable and some have more. **Pig** has one syllable.
Chicken has two. Can you think of another word that has two syllables?
Sounding out each syllable at a time will help you sound out longer,
unfamiliar words.

➡ READ the words in the box. Use those words to FILL IN the lines to
complete the story.

| bunny carrot scarecrow pumpkins garden farmer |
| apples summer harvest fiddle |

_____ is over and fall is here. It is _____ time! Ripe red

_____ are ready for picking. The _____ is bursting with

vegetables. Hop, hop, hop! A _____ tries to steal a bright orange

_____. "Go away!" cries the _____. A _____ watches

over the fields. Corn, _____, and squash need to be picked, too.

At the end of a busy day, the farmer will play her _____ as the sun

sets over the farm.

SKILL: Letter Patterns

9. Dividing Line

Some words have two vowel sounds separated by only one consonant, making a **v**owel, **c**onsonant, **v**owel (**vcv**) pattern. If the first vowel sound is long, divide the word into syllables *before* the consonant (**v | c**) as in the word **su | per**. If the vowel sound is short, divide the word *after* the consonant (**vc | v**) as in the word **trav | el**.

➡ READ the words out loud. CLAP your hands for each syllable. CIRCLE the choice that shows a line dividing the word into syllables correctly. WRITE the word to show the two syllables.

1. **pilot**   pi | lot   pil | ot   _____ | _____

2. **dragon**   dra | gon   drag | on   _____ | _____

3. **cabin**   ca | bin   cab | in   _____ | _____

4. **frozen**   fro | zen   froz | en   _____ | _____

5. **salad**   sa | lad   sal |ad   _____ | _____

6. **pirate**   pi | rate   pir | ate   _____ | _____

7. **music**   mu | sic   mus | ic   _____ | _____

8. **apron**   a | pron   ap | ron   _____ | _____

9. **paper**   pa | per   pap | er   _____ | _____

10. **hotel**   ho | tel   hot | el   _____ | _____

SKILL: Letter Patterns

10. Tiger vs. Camel

In a two-syllable word that has a **v**owel, **c**onsonant, **v**owel (**vcv**) pattern, divide the word into syllables after the first vowel if it has a long sound (**v | cv**).

If the vowel has a short sound, divide the word after the consonant (**vc | v**). The word *tiger* follows the **v | cv** pattern. The word *camel* follows the **vc | v** pattern. The line is here for you to practice, but remember, it doesn't appear in a written word.

➡ READ each word in the box. CLAP your hands for each syllable. Use the **v | cv** pattern rule to divide the word into syllables. WRITE the word on the lines under the correct pattern.

| begin   never   baker   open   spider   lemon   acorn   visit   music |
| paper   seven   damage   even   habit   Friday   flavor   planet |
| money   talent   palace |

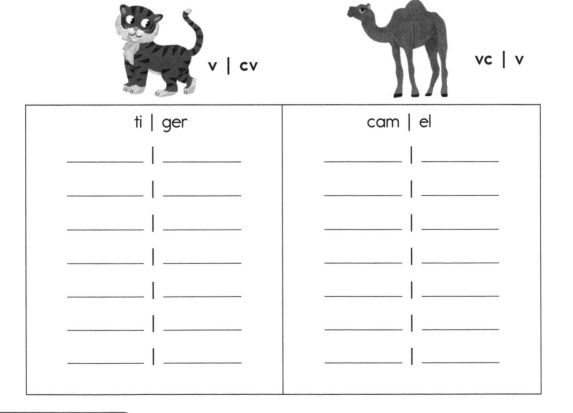

v | cv   vc | v

ti | ger	cam | el
_____ | _____	_____ | _____
_____ | _____	_____ | _____
_____ | _____	_____ | _____
_____ | _____	_____ | _____
_____ | _____	_____ | _____
_____ | _____	_____ | _____
_____ | _____	_____ | _____

SKILL: Letter Patterns

11. Prefix Preview

You can build new words out of existing words. Words that can be added to are called **base words** (or sometimes **root words**). When a **prefix** is added to the beginning of a base word, it creates a new word with its own meaning. Here are some common prefixes and their meanings:

un- not, opposite

in- not or in

re- do again

pre- before

dis- opposite

mis- wrong

➡ READ each word in the box. WRITE the word next to its meaning.

> unclean   misspell   unhappy   redo   reappear   disobey
> incomplete   misbehave   dishonest   preheat

1. not happy _____

2. not complete _____

3. behave the wrong way _____

4. appear again _____

5. not clean _____

6. not obey _____

7. spell the wrong way _____

8. heat before _____

9. not honest _____

10. do again _____

SKILL: Prefixes and Suffixes

12. Unafraid!

When a prefix is added to a base word, it changes the meaning of the word.
➡ READ each word in the picture. COLOR each section using the color in the key that matches the prefix in the word.

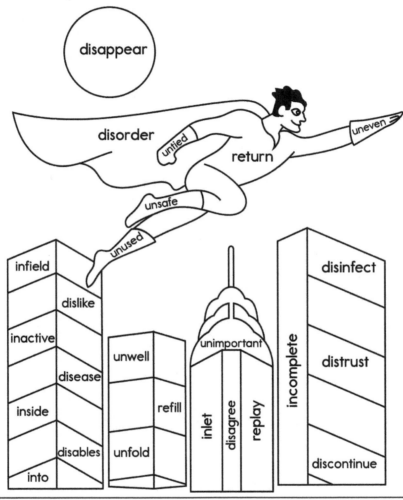

un	**Prefix un-:** unafraid, unimportant, untie, unable, uneven, unwell, unused, unlock, unfold, unlucky, unsafe
re	**Prefix re-:** replay, recycle, return, reheat, refill, rewrite, rebuild, relocate, rename, repaint, retell
dis	**Prefix dis-:** disappear, discontinue, disorder, disinfect, distrust, dislike, disagree, disable
in	**Prefix in-:** infield, incomplete, inactive, invisible, inlet, into, inside

SKILL: Prefixes and Suffixes

13. Super Suffixes

A base word can be built on by adding a **suffix** to the end. The new word will have a new meaning. Here are some common suffixes and their meanings:

s or **-es** more than one

-ing happening now

-ed already happened

-er more

-est most

-**ful** full of

-**less** without

-**y** full of

-**ly** in a certain way

➡ READ each sentence. COLOR the bubble next to the suffix that finishes the word to best complete the sentence. WRITE the suffix next to the word.

1. The artist paint_____ a picture of a great white shark last week.
   ⚪ ful   ⚪ s   ⚪ es   ⚪ ed

2. The universe is decorated with an end_____ number of stars.
   ⚪ ing   ⚪ ly   ⚪ less   ⚪ est

3. Please tiptoe quiet_____ so that you don't wake the baby.
   ⚪ est   ⚪ ly   ⚪ ful   ⚪ es

4. How many book_____ have you read this summer?
   ⚪ ing   ⚪ s   ⚪ less   ⚪ ed

5. The more books you read, the smart_____ you will be!
   ⚪ ful   ⚪ er   ⚪ less   ⚪ es

6. The giraffe is the tall_____ animal in the zoo.
   ⚪ y   ⚪ s   ⚪ est   ⚪ er

7. Antonio brought home three play_____ puppies.
   ⚪ er   ⚪ ing   ⚪ ly   ⚪ ful

8. The fairy granted him three wish_____.
   ⚪ es   ⚪ ly   ⚪ ing   ⚪ ful

9. After practice, the baseball players are sweat_____.
   ⚪ ful   ⚪ y   ⚪ ly   ⚪ est

10. The chorus is sing_____ my favorite song.
    ⚪ ly   ⚪ s   ⚪ ing   ⚪ est

SKILL: Prefixes and Suffixes

14. Beginnings and Endings

A **prefix** is a letter or group of letters added to the beginning of a word. A **suffix** is a letter or group of letters added to the end of a word. Both give the word a new meaning.

➡ READ each word. COLOR the box **red** if the word has a prefix. COLOR the box **blue** if the word has a suffix. Three in a row is tic-tac-toe!

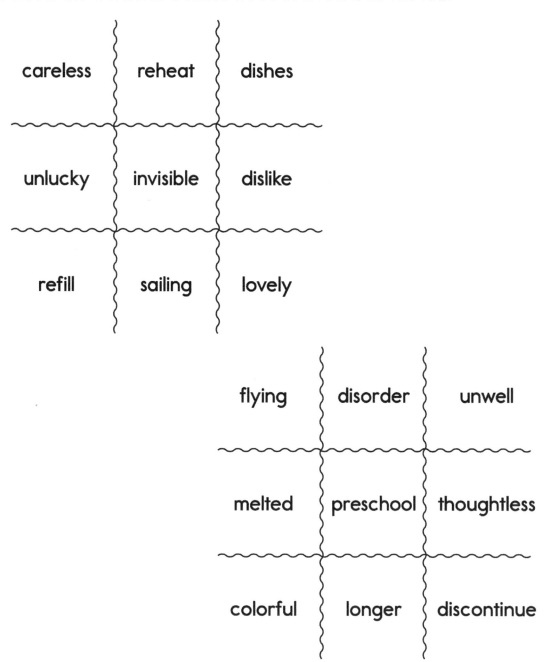

careless	reheat	dishes
unlucky	invisible	dislike
refill	sailing	lovely

flying	disorder	unwell
melted	preschool	thoughtless
colorful	longer	discontinue

SKILL: Prefixes and Suffixes

15. Do You Hear a Bear?

Sometimes words don't follow the rules. The **oo** in **moon** does not sound the same as the **oo** in **book**. It is important to be able to spot these differences so you can recognize words that show up often as you read.

➡ LOOK at each picture. COMPLETE each word below using the letter choices in the box.

| oo ou ie ow ea |

1. b __ __ r

2. sn __ __

3. t__ __ ch

4. m __ __ n

5. s __ __ p

6. t __ __ r

7. t __ __

8. b __ __ k

9. p __ __ ce

10. c __ __

11. h __ __ r

12. l __ __ d

SKILL: Spelling Patterns

16. Mother Robin's Nest

Key details in a story give readers important information. They answer the questions **who**, **what**, **where**, **when**, **why**, and **how**.

➡ READ the story and then READ each question. WRITE the answer to each question.

The snow has melted and buds are sprouting on the trees. Spring is here! Mother Robin needs to build a nest. She needs a safe and comfortable place to lay her eggs. She finds the perfect tree for her nest. Piece by piece, she collects soft grass and twigs and presses them into a cup shape. When her nest is finished, she will lay her eggs and wait for them to hatch!

1. **Who** is the story about?

_____

2. **What** is Mother Robin doing?

_____

3. **Where** will the nest be built?

_____

4. **When** will the nest be built?

_____

5. **Why** does Mother Robin need to build a nest?

_____

6. **How** will the nest be built?

_____

SKILL: Key Details

17. A Dog for Geo

Key details give readers important information. They tell you the main ideas:
who, **what**, **where**, **when**, **why**, and **how**.

➡ READ the story. COLOR the bubble next to the correct answer to
each question.

Geo loves dogs. Every year, he asks his parents for a dog. Every year they
say, "No, you are too young to take care of a dog." When he turns nine,
Geo decides that this year will be different. He will show
his parents that he is responsible. He reads books
about pet care. When their neighbor goes on
vacation, he feeds her dog. When Uncle Leo
breaks his leg, he offers to walk his dog. A week
before he turns ten, Geo asks his parents for a
dog. This time their answer is different. On Geo's
tenth birthday, his parents take him to the animal
shelter to adopt a dog.

1. Who is the story about?
   ○ Geo's parents   ○ Uncle Leo   ○ Geo

2. What does Geo want for his birthday?
   ○ a present   ○ a dog   ○ a party

3. Why don't Geo's parents want to give him a dog?
   ○ They don't like dogs.   ○ Geo is allergic to dogs.
   ○ They think Geo is too young to care for a dog.

4. How does Geo show his parents that he is old enough to take care
   of a dog?
   ○ Geo begs his parents. ○ Geo plays with dogs at the park
   ○ Geo takes care of other dogs.

5. Where do Geo's parents bring him to get the dog?
   ○ the animal shelter   ○ the neighbor's house   ○ the pet shop

6. When does Geo get his dog?
   ○ when he is nine   ○ on his tenth birthday   ○ never

SKILL: Key Details

18. The Lion and the Mouse

The **main topic**, or **main idea**, tells what a story is about. **Fables** are short stories that teach a lesson or moral about life. In a fable, the **lesson** is the main topic.

➡ READ the fable. CIRCLE the picture that shows the main topic. Then CIRCLE the lesson that the story teaches below.

One day as Lion napped, his snore startled Mouse as she walked by. In a hurry to get away, Mouse ran right over Lion's nose and woke him up. Lion trapped Mouse in his sharp claws. Mouse begged to be let go and promised to repay Lion if he released her. Lion laughed at the idea of such a small creature ever helping him but agreed to let Mouse go. A week later, Mouse heard an angry roar. Lion was trapped in a hunter's net! Mouse gnawed on the ropes until Lion was free. "Thank you!" said Lion. "Even though you are small, you are a big help!"

➡ CIRCLE the lesson that the story teaches.

Always tell the truth.

Never hurt anyone.

You are never too small to be a big help.

Teamwork will get the job done.

SKILL: Main Topic

19. Telling Tales

Every story or text has a **main topic**, or **main idea**. Texts are organized into smaller parts called **paragraphs**. Each paragraph has a **focus** that supports the main topic of the story. A story can have one paragraph or many.
➡ READ the paragraphs on the left. DRAW a line to connect each paragraph to its **main topic** on the right.

Folktales are stories that are told over and over again. They are passed down from parents to children over the years. Each time the story is told, it changes a little bit. Every country has its own stories, but the lessons they teach are often the same.

A fable is a kind of folktale. Fables are short stories that teach lessons or morals about life. The characters are usually animals that think or act like people. *Aesop's Fables* is a famous collection of fables known throughout the world.

Fairy tales are magical folktales about good vs. evil. They are often set in lands far away where magical things happen. Fairy tales usually have royal or make-believe characters such as dragons, fairies, or giants. These stories teach lessons and end with the good characters living happily ever after.

Fairy tales are magical stories about good vs. evil.

Folktales are stories that are retold many times.

Fables are short folktales that teach a life lesson or moral.

SKILL: Main Topic

20. Sharp Focus

The **focus** is the most important idea in a paragraph. All of the paragraphs in a story must also support the **main topic** of the story.

➡ READ the story and then READ the topics. WRITE the topic that best describes each paragraph in the space above.

Paragraph 1: _____

The Statue of Liberty wears a pointed crown and holds a torch high above her head. People all over the world recognize her as a symbol of freedom. She stands as tall as a skyscraper on a small island in New York Harbor. The statue was a gift of friendship from France more than a hundred years ago.

Paragraph 2: _____

A French sculptor named Frédéric-Auguste Bartholdi designed the Statue of Liberty. It took more than ten years to build. The statue was built in France. It was so big that it had to be taken apart before it was shipped to the United States. Once it arrived, it took several months to put back together.

Paragraph 3: _____

Millions of people visit the Statue of Liberty every year. The only way to get there is by ferryboat. Visitors can take guided tours, explore a museum, and even climb up the statue. There are almost four hundred stairs to climb to reach the crown, but the view is worth the hike!

Building the Statue of Liberty   A Great Gift from France

The Statue of Liberty Stands for Freedom   Visiting the Statue of Liberty

Riding on a Ferry

SKILL: Focus

21. Very Inventive

Every story or text has a **main topic**, or **main idea**. Each paragraph within the story has a **focus** that supports the main topic.

➼ READ the text. COLOR the bubble next to the correct answer for each question below.

Paragraph 1

An invention is something new that someone makes. Most of the time an invention is created because of a need. Many inventions have changed the way people live. Can you imagine life without cars, electricity, or plastic?

Paragraph 2

Many inventions have been built over time. The wheel, spear, knife, and arrow are some of the earliest inventions. As new technology and materials become available, inventions can be improved and added to. Wheels, carts, carriages, bikes, cars . . . what will come next?

Paragraph 3

Sometimes inventions happen by accident. One day, young Frank Epperson stirred a cup of powdered juice and accidently left it outside. Overnight, the temperature fell and the juice froze. The next day, Epperson pulled on the spoon and out came the first Popsicle ever! Chocolate chip cookies, matches, and microwave ovens were also accidental inventions.

1. What is the main topic of the text?
   - ⚪ famous inventors
   - ⚪ inventions
   - ⚪ cars and phones
   - ⚪ accidental inventions

2. What is the focus of paragraph 1?
   - ⚪ introducing inventions
   - ⚪ life without inventions
   - ⚪ famous inventors
   - ⚪ filling a need

3. What is the focus of paragraph 2?
   - ⚪ early inventions
   - ⚪ wheels and carts
   - ⚪ materials used for inventions
   - ⚪ inventions build on each other

4. What is the focus of paragraph 3?
   - ⚪ Popsicles
   - ⚪ Frank Epperson's great idea
   - ⚪ accidental inventions
   - ⚪ great ideas

SKILL: Focus

22. Focus Finder

Stories and texts have **main topics**. They can have one paragraph or many. Each paragraph has a **focus** that is connected to the main idea of the story. ➡️ READ all three passages. CIRCLE the paragraph number (or numbers) that matches the correct focus. (More than one paragraph may match.)

Paragraph 1

Community helpers are a part of our everyday lives. They live and work in our community. Their work helps make the community a nice place to live, work, and play. Our lives are made better because of the work they do.

Paragraph 2

There are many kinds of community helpers. Firefighters and police officers help keep our community safe. Doctors and nurses help people feel better when they are sick. Teachers and librarians help people learn. Bakers, farmers, and cashiers sell us things we need and want. Electricians and plumbers fix things. All these jobs help the people in the community in some way.

Paragraph 3

Community helpers can also be volunteers who help in their free time. Cleaning up litter, planting trees, and reading to senior citizens are ways that volunteers help the places they live. Kids can help, too! They can walk dogs, recycle cans, and donate their old toys and books to younger children. You are never too old or too young to help your community.

1. Community helpers of all ages can volunteer in their communities.   **1   2   3   All**

2. Community helpers make their communities better in some way.   **1   2   3   All**

3. There are many kinds of community helpers.
   1   2   3   All

4. Community helpers are a part of our everyday lives.
   1   2   3   All

SKILL: Focus

23. Saving the Everglades

When one event causes another event to happen, it is called **cause and effect**. The **cause** is *why* something happened. The **effect** is *what* happened as a result.

➡ READ the passage. DRAW a line to connect each **cause** to its matching **effect** below.

The Everglades is a huge wetland area in southern Florida. There is no place on Earth quite like it. It is home to many kinds of plants and animals, including birds, alligators, manatees, and the rare Florida panther. In the early 1900s, people began to drain the area to build houses and cities. They thought that the Everglades was a useless swamp. Marjory Stoneman Douglas disagreed. Without the Everglades, the plants and animals that lived there would have no home. She believed that the Everglades should be protected. She gave speeches, wrote articles, and published a book about why this special area was important. People listened to her ideas. Marjory's work helped turn the area into a national park. Everglades National Park was formed in 1947 to protect the plants and animals living there. Marjory felt that everyone had a responsibility to help protect nature. For the rest of her life, she continued working to save more land around the park.

Causes

Many people believed that the Everglades was a useless swamp.

Marjory Stoneman Douglas gave speeches and wrote about how important it was to protect the Everglades.

Cities and houses were built on Everglades land.

Effects

Everglades National Park was created.

The land was drained to build houses and cities.

The animals were losing their homes.

SKILL: Connecting Ideas

24. Basketball Now and Then

You can connect ideas and events by thinking about how they are the same or different. **Comparing** shows how two or more things are alike. **Contrasting** shows how they are different.

➡ READ the passage. WRITE two ways that basketball is the same as it used to be where the circles overlap. WRITE two differences between basketball then and now in each outside part of the circle.

In 1891, Dr. James Naismith invented the game of basketball. Originally, there were 13 rules. Now, there are more than 100! Early games were played with peach baskets. If a player got the ball into the basket, someone had to climb a ladder to get it out. The original baskets were replaced with wire hoops and nets that allow the ball to fall through. At first the game was played with however many people showed up to play. Today, only five players from each team can play at a time. The game was first played with a soccer ball, but it was difficult to dribble. Now special balls are made just for basketball. Rules for passing have not changed over time. In the early games, the courts had no boundaries. This didn't work well when players chased after balls that landed in the stands! Now, courts have boundary lines. Basketball has been a popular sport to play and watch since it was invented.

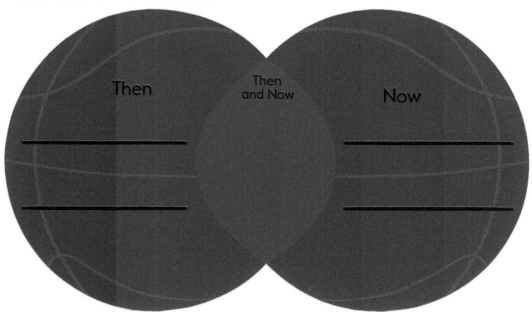

SKILL: Connecting Ideas

25. A Treat for the Birds

Step-by-step written instructions tell the reader how to make or do something. Instructions and recipes show a **sequence** of steps to follow when you are making something.

➡ READ the instructions for making a bird feeder. DRAW a circle around the words that tell the order of the steps. WRITE the number under the picture to correspond with the order of steps in the instructions.

Materials

12-inch piece of string	craft stick
pine cone	¼ cup of bird seed
½ cup of peanut butter	small bowl

To make a pine cone bird feeder, first tie the string around the top of the pine cone. Next, spread the peanut butter all over the surface of the pine cone using the craft stick. After that, pour the birdseed into the bowl and roll the pine cone over the birdseed. Last, hang your feeder on a branch near a window so you can watch the birds come to the feeder.

_____   _____   _____   _____

SKILL: Connecting Ideas

26. Gold Rush

A **problem** is a challenge, obstacle, or something that goes wrong. A
solution is how it is solved or fixed. In many stories, there is a problem and
then one or more solutions.

➡ READ the text. DRAW a line to connect the problem to the best solution.

In the late 1840s, gold was discovered in California. Thousands of people
rushed to the area, hoping to become rich by mining for gold. When they
arrived, they needed many supplies. They needed tents, bedding, and food
to set up camp. They also needed pans, picks, and shovels to hunt for gold.
At the time, there weren't many places to buy supplies. Merchants started
businesses to sell supplies. One of these merchants was Levi Strauss.

   One of Levi Strauss's customers was a tailor named Jacob Davis. He
bought fabric to make pants for miners. Digging for gold was rough
work. The miners' pants quickly wore out or ripped at the seams. Mr.
Davis solved the problem. He placed brass rivets in places where seams
often ripped. More and more people wanted his pants, but he didn't have
enough money to grow his business. He asked Mr. Strauss for help. The
two men teamed up to manufacture the pants. They made the pants out
of sturdy denim fabric. The pants became very popular. The business
grew and grew. Although some gold seekers did find their fortunes,
many did not. The businesspeople who sold to the miners often became
wealthier than the miners.

Problems

| The gold seekers needed supplies. |

| Miners often ripped their pants. |

| Mr. Davis didn't have enough
money to grow his business. |

Solutions

| Mr. Davis teamed up with
Mr. Strauss to manufacture
pants for miners. |

| Mr. Davis invented sturdy pants. |

| Merchants opened businesses that
sold supplies that miners needed. |

SKILL: Connecting Ideas

27. Best Camping Trip Ever

Stories are often organized to have a clear **beginning**, a **middle**, and an **end**. The beginning introduces the characters, setting, and problem. In the middle, the characters try to solve the problem. In the end, the problem gets solved.

➡ This story is all mixed up! NUMBER the parts in the correct order to organize the story.

_____ Dad had an idea. He suggested camping inside.

_____ Just before they packed the car, the sky turned dark and gray. A crack of thunder shook the house. It was followed by a streak of lightning and pouring rain.

_____ "This is the best camping trip ever!" said Shen. Everyone agreed. "Can we do it again next weekend?" asked Lee, just before she fell asleep.

_____ All week long, Shen and Lee were looking forward to going camping with their parents. Their bags were packed, and they were ready to go.

_____ They set up their tent in the living room and roasted marshmallows in the fireplace. Mom played her guitar, and everyone sang along.

_____ Everyone was disappointed. Now they couldn't go camping.

SKILL: Structure

28. A Day with Balloons

Stories have a **structure**. The structure is the way a story is planned or organized. Fiction stories have a **beginning**, a **middle**, and an **end**.
➡ READ the story. DRAW a line to connect each part of the story to its matching picture.

1. Teeny Tiny woke up on the day of her party to find ten brightly colored balloons tied to the end of her bed.

2. After breakfast, she tied the balloons around her wrist. She wanted to share her balloons with her friends at school.

3. As soon as she stepped out the door, she went up. Up, up, up, she soared. She flew over her house and over the school. "Help!" she cried.

4. A bird came to her rescue. He plucked one balloon and gave it to her friend Meg. Teeny Tiny sank a little lower. The bird plucked another balloon and gave it to Frida. Teeny Tiny sank lower. Again and again, the bird helped pass the balloons to the friends as Teeny Tiny sank lower and lower.

5. Teeny Tiny finally sank to the ground holding one last balloon. Her friends were happy with their balloons. "This was the most exciting day ever, but I think I have had enough excitement to last a whole year," said Teeny Tiny as she gave her last balloon to her new friend, the bird.

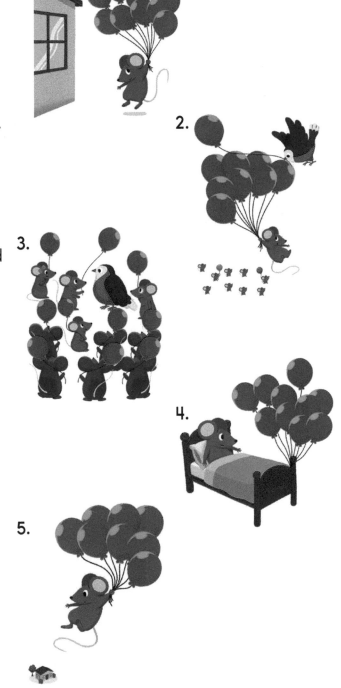

1.

2.

3.

4.

5.

SKILL: Structure

29. Alliteration Alphabet

Alliteration is when two or more nearby words have the same beginning sound. Writers often use alliteration to create the rhythm and structure in poetry. Here are some **alliterative sentences** you may be familiar with:

She sells seashells by the seashore.

Peter Piper picked a peck of pickled peppers.

➡ FILL IN the blanks to make alliterative sentences.

1. Aunt Abigail always ate _____.

2. Byron Brown _____ brownies.

3. Cute cats climb _____ crocodiles.

4. Debbie's dad devours _____ donuts.

5. Every evening, Emily _____.

6. Gordon gives grapes to _____.

7. Helen hikes _____.

8. Josie jets to _____.

9. Lazy lizards leap over laughing _____.

10. Sam sips _____ smoothies.

11. Tina tickled ten tiny _____.

12. Zebras zip to _____.

13. _____ mice miss _____ monkeys.

14. Nervous Nancy never _____.

15. Perfect _____ pick _____.

BONUS! Try writing an alliterative sentence using your name.

30. Dear Diary

A **narrator** is the person telling a story. Sometimes it's the author or a character the author has created. **Point of view** is the perspective (beliefs, feelings, and ideas) of the narrator. Each narrator has their own **voice**, or their unique style and tone of talking.

➡ Tina and Marina are twins. READ each diary entry. CIRCLE the character that matches the point of view in each sentence below.

Dear Diary,
The amusement park was so much fun! My favorite ride is the roller coaster. I love the thrilling feeling before it zips down. The water at the beach was too cold! I started to shiver after a minute. We built a sandcastle, but a hermit crab almost pinched me! I screamed and raced back to the towel. We had yummy hot dogs for dinner. It was the best day all summer!

 Love,
 Tina

Dear Diary,
The amusement park was scary! I didn't like the roller coaster at all. It made my stomach drop every time it zipped down. The afternoon was so much fun! The water was the perfect temperature. I swam for an hour! Afterward, we built a sandcastle with a pool for the cute little hermit crabs. We had delicious hot dogs for dinner. It was the best day all summer!

 Sincerely yours,
 Marina

1. The roller coaster was a scary ride.   **Tina**   **Marina**   **both**

2. It was the best day all summer.   **Tina**   **Marina**   **both**

3. The hermit crabs were scary.   **Tina**   **Marina**   **both**

4. The water was the perfect temperature. **Tina**   **Marina**   **both**

5. The hot dogs were delicious.   **Tina**   **Marina**   **both**

SKILL: Voice

31. City Mouse, Country Mouse

A narrator or character's **point of view** is their feelings, beliefs, and ideas. Sometimes the characters in a story have different points of view. Each character's point of view helps create their **voice**.

➡ READ the story. WRITE three things you know about each character's **point of view** under their picture.

One day, City Mouse went to visit her cousin in the country for a picnic. She wore her finest gown and hat. A horse galloped by and kicked up a cloud of dust. Terrified, City Mouse gasped and brushed off her fancy dress.

"How can anyone live in such a frightening, dirty place?" she wondered.

As they ate, City Mouse sniffed at the hard cheese, lettuce, and wheat. "Do you have any marmalade?" she asked her cousin.

"No," replied Country Mouse. "Our food is simple and nourishing."

"Tomorrow, you must come to visit me and try some fancy city food!" said City Mouse.

The next day, Country Mouse traveled to the city. She wore a simple dress and a straw hat. Along the way, a taxi sprayed her with a puddle as it sped by.

"How can anyone live in such a scary, dirty place?" She thought. At her cousin's apartment, a table was spread with frosted cakes and pastries.

"See, isn't this fancy city food better than simple country food?" asked City Mouse.

"It *is* very tasty," agreed Country Mouse. To herself she thought, "But I *do* have a bit of a stomachache!"

1. _____
2. _____
3. _____

1. _____
2. _____
3. _____

32. Life in the Forest

Readers can use **context clues** to help them figure out the
meaning of unfamiliar words. The words you know around a
word you don't know are the clues that can help.

➡ READ each sentence. DRAW a line to connect the words
in **bold** to their meaning.

1. You will know that a skunk is near before you
   see it. The horrible **odor** will hurt your nose
   and make your eyes water.

2. It is difficult to see a great horned owl sleeping in its nest. Their brown feather patterns
   are **camouflaged** to match the bark of
   the tree.

3. Bats are **nocturnal**. When the sun sets, they fly
   off to look for their breakfast.

4. Do you hear a red-tailed hawk, a bald eagle,
   or a blue jay? It's hard to tell. Sometimes blue
   jays **mimic** the calls of other birds.

5. Beavers **gnaw** on young trees and then drag
   them to ponds to build their homes.

6. Mountain lions are **carnivores**. They eat rab-
   bits, mice, and other animals. Plants are not a
   part of their diet.

7. A moose is **massive**. Next to a moose, a person
   looks very small.

8. Woodchucks **hibernate** during the winter. They
   don't wake up until the weather starts to warm
   up in the spring.

a. huge

b. meat eaters

c. sleep deeply

d. chew

e. copy

f. disguised

g. smell

h. awake at night

SKILL: Relevant Text

33. Look for the Clues!

Context clues in a sentence or passage can help you figure out the meaning of unknown words.

➡ READ the passage. COLOR the bubble with the meaning of the **bold** words.

Deserts are the driest habitats on Earth. It seldom rains in the desert. Many deserts get less than 10 inches of precipitation a year. Some deserts are scorching hot during the day and freezing cold at night. Some deserts are always cold. Many people think that nothing can live in such an arid landscape, but that is not true. Desert plants and animals have adapted to survive without much water. Cacti are plants that can store enough water in their stems to last until the next rainfall. Many animals get water from the foods they eat. Kangaroo rats get moisture from the seeds they eat. Meat-eating coyotes get liquid from their prey. Camels quickly gulp down and store large amounts of water when they have the opportunity.

1. **precipitation**
   O heat   O temperature   O rain

2. **scorching**
   O very   O sizzling   O heat

3. **arid**
   O dry   O rainy   O hot

4. **adapted**
   O grown   O lived   O changed

5. **store**
   O hold or keep   O carry   O place to buy things

6. **moisture**
   O food   O water   O nourishment

7. **prey**
   O food   O animals killed to eat   O rabbit

8. **opportunity**
   O idea   O time   O chance

SKILL: Relevant Text

34. Solar System Study

A **glossary** is a list of important words and their definitions. It is usually located at the back of a book. Books that have a glossary are usually nonfiction. **Nonfiction** means that the information is factual. The words in a glossary are listed alphabetically to make them easy to locate.

➡ READ this glossary from a book about the solar system. Use the glossary to FILL IN the word that completes the sentences about the solar system.

Glossary	
astronaut	a person who travels into space
gravity	a force that pulls things together
moon	large round object that travels around Earth
orbit	the path of one object as it goes around another object
planet	a large object that travels around a star
solar system	the sun and everything that travels around it
telescope	a tool that makes faraway objects appear closer
universe	everything that exists

1. The _____ is planning a trip to the moon.

2. A large object that travels around a star is a _____.

3. A _____ will help you see faraway planets.

4. The _____ is a large round object that orbits Earth.

5. The solar system is part of the _____

6. The force that pulls people to Earth is called _____.

SKILL: Nonfiction Text

35. Special Features

Text features help readers better understand nonfiction texts.

➡ READ and COLOR the bubble next to the text feature shown in the box.

Cheetahs can reach a speed of 50 to 80 miles an hour.

○ diagram   ○ caption   ○ heading

---

flower   produces seeds or pollen so the plant can reproduce

leaf   makes food for the plant from the sun

root   anchors the plant to the ground and soaks up water from the soil

stem   supports a plant and carries minerals and water to all parts of
          the plant

○ index   ○ table of contents   ○ glossary

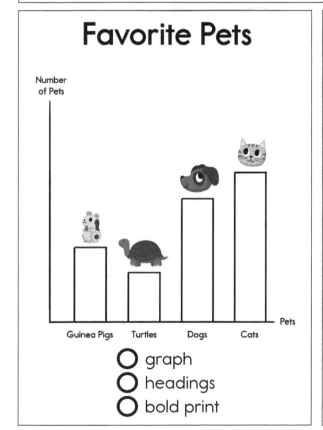

Favorite Pets

Number of Pets

Guinea Pigs   Turtles   Dogs   Cats   Pets

○ graph
○ headings
○ bold print

Introduction 3
Welcoming the Seasons 5
Winter Fun 10
Super Spring 20
Sizzling Summer 30
Fabulous Fall 40

○ index
○ table of contents
○ headings

SKILL: Nonfiction Text

36. Recycled Reasons

Have you ever thought about *why* an author writes? Authors write for a reason. As you read, try to think of what the **author's purpose** might be. Is it to **inform** or teach their readers about a topic, to **entertain** their readers, or to **persuade** their readers to agree with them or to do something?
➡ READ each passage. DRAW a line to connect the passage to the author's purpose.

Recycling

> Recycling turns trash into things that can be used again.
> It takes energy and resources to make just about anything.
> Recycling uses less energy and fewer resources. When you
> recycle, you are helping the planet and everyone on it!

Mayville Recycles

inform

> Please help Mayville help our planet! Please sort your trash
> into plastic, glass, and paper. These items will be recycled.
> Consider composting food scraps at home. This will help
> reduce the amount of garbage that is sent to landfills. We
> hope you will join your neighbors in doing your part to help.

entertain

Ruth Recycles

> "There's nothing to do!" pouted Ruth one rainy afternoon.
> "You can come with me to the store to buy a present
> for Grandma's birthday," said Mom, "but first we have to
> recycle these cans and bottles." As Ruth helped her mom,
> she got an idea. "We could make Grandma a bird feeder
> out of an old plastic bottle," she said. Ruth and her mom
> had a fun afternoon making Grandma's present. "We
> saved money *and* helped save the planet," said Ruth.

persuade

SKILL: Author's Purpose

37. Reading the Clues

Pictures add information to a text. They give clues that help you better understand the characters, setting, or plot.

➡ LOOK at each picture and READ the sentences. CIRCLE the **bold** word below that best completes the sentence.

Emi played outside for a long time.

Sally's dog barked.

The hummingbird drank nectar from its favorite-color flower.

1. I know that the season is

_____.

fall   winter
spring   summer

2. The dog is barking

_____.

quietly   fiercely
silently   loudly

3. The hummingbird's favorite color

is _____.

blue   green
brown   white

Sean was the fastest athlete on his team.

Grandma and Grandpa love the view from their new house.

Baby is tired.

4. The boy is on a

_____ team.

hockey   soccer
gymnastics   swim

5. Grandma and Grandpa's new house looks out over the _____.

river   mountains
ocean   lake

6. The part of the day

is _____.

morning   noon
night   sunset

SKILL: Picture Clues

38. Sly Sam

Pictures often give the reader information that is not in the story. They add information to the characters, setting, and plot.

➡ READ the story. LOOK at the picture. COLOR the bubble next to the correct answer for each question below.

The Diaz family had a problem. Some of their things had gone missing!

"Has anyone seen my reading glasses?" asked Mom. No one had.

"I can't find my car keys!" exclaimed Dad.

"I haven't used them," replied Mom.

"Where's my paintbrush?" asked Cheryl. No one knew where it had gone.

"I must have misplaced my earbuds!" said Burt.

"Oh dear!" said Grandma, "I don't know what I've done with my hearing aids."

Spot whimpered. He couldn't find his bone. Everyone looked and looked but couldn't find any of the missing items. All the while, Sam slept peacefully on the couch.

"Wake up, Sam!" Everyone cried, "We need your help!" Sam opened one eye, stretched, and went back to sleep. No one knew what to do. They had looked *everywhere* for the missing things.

1. Who is Sam?
   O a boy   O a dog   O a cat

2. What does the word **sly** in the title mean?
   O sneaky   O silly   O unhelpful

3. Who took the missing things?
   O a robber   O Sam   O no one knows

4. Where are the missing things?
   O no one knows   O in the car   O under the couch cushion

SKILL: Picture Clues

39. Blow, Wind, Blow!

Diagrams are pictures with labels that help explain a text.

➡ READ the passage. UNSCRAMBLE the words to solve the riddles below.

Around and around the blades of a wind turbine spin, turning wind into electricity. Taller than a 30-story building, with blades longer than a blue whale, wind turbines tower over the landscape. They look like they could be gigantic fans, but they work the opposite way. Fans use electricity to make wind, and turbines use wind to make electricity. As wind spins the blades, the blades turn a shaft and gears that are connected to a generator. The generator turns this movement into electricity. The electricity gets sent through lines to a substation and then to houses and buildings. Wind farms have many wind turbines. They can provide enough electricity for entire communities. Using wind energy is becoming more and more popular because it doesn't pollute the air and water. It is a renewable energy source that won't run out. Nature replaces it all the time!

1. I can make electricity out of wind! What am I?

   dniw rtubnie   __ __ __ __   __ __ __ __ __ __ __

2. I turn movement into energy. What am I?

   enerratog   __ __ __ __ __ __ __ __ __

3. We are places with many turbines. What are we?

   dinw sarmf   __ __ __ __   __ __ __ __ __

4. We are longer than a blue whale. What are we?

   seadlb   __ __ __ __ __ __ __ __ __

5. You can make me out of wind. What am I?

   eeccttiilry   __ __ __ __ __ __ __ __ __

6. We need electricity to make wind. What are we?

   anfs   __ __ __

SKILL: Picture Clues

40. What Kind of Pie?

Charts, graphs, and diagrams can help you better understand a text.
➡ READ the passage and LOOK at the chart. WRITE the answers to the questions below.

Mr. Kim told his cooking class that they were going to bake pies next week. He asked the class what kind of pie they should make. Everyone's hand went up in the air. Apple, peach, blueberry, lemon meringue, chocolate cream; everyone seemed to want a different kind of pie! Mr. Kim told the class that they would have to choose *one* kind of pie. He decided to take a survey. Each young chef could vote for their favorite kind of pie. They would bake the pie that had the most votes next week. Mr. Kim wrote the names of five different kinds of pie on the whiteboard. He then asked everyone to write their favorite kind on a piece of paper. Mr. Kim counted the votes. He drew a big circle on the board. He sectioned the circle into slices of pie. The sections were different sizes. Each slice had the name of one of the choices on it. He explained that he had made a pie chart using their votes. The pie chart was a kind of graph that showed the results of the survey. Now everyone knew what kind of pie they would bake next week!

1. What kind of pie will the class bake next week? _____

2. How many children are in Mr. Kim's class? _____

3. What kind of pie was the second favorite in the class? _____

4. What problem do you think Mr. Kim will have if he tells his class that they will be making pizza the following week? _____

   _____

5. What could Mr. Kim do to solve the problem? _____

   _____

SKILL: Picture Clues

41. Kindness Matters

An **author's view** is how they feel about a topic. In their writing, they share the reasons for their feelings.

➡ READ the passage. THINK about how the author feels about being kind. DRAW a picture that shows how you could be kind to someone.

Kindness is a wonderful gift that costs nothing to give. Being kind is a gentle, thoughtful, understanding way of acting toward someone else. If someone is having a bad day, a simple smile can help them feel better. That was easy! Saying something nice is another way to be kind. It shows the other person that you noticed something good about them. That's a happy feeling! Being helpful is kind. It makes another person's day easier. Kindness connects you to other people in a good way. When you think of how you would feel if you were in someone else's situation, it is easy to find ways to be kind. If you saw a new kid sitting alone at the playground, you could invite them to play. Soon, you would both have a new friend! Being kind gives you a happy feeling in return. Simply being kind makes the world a better place to be.

SKILL: Author's View

42. Festival of Colors

Reading about a topic from different sources can help you learn a lot! As you read, **compare and contrast** important information. *Compare* means to look for how things are the same. *Contrast* means to look for differences.

➥ READ the two passages. COLOR the bubble next to each question to show where you would find the answer. WRITE the answer to the question on the line below. FILL IN the Venn diagram with what you've learned.

All About Holi

Happy Holi! Spring is here! Holi is a joyful Indian festival that marks the beginning of spring. It is also known as the "Festival of Colors." It is a time for new beginnings, friendship, and lots of fun. The celebration begins with a bonfire on Holi eve. People gather to sing, dance, and eat sweets. The following day, people greet each other with a rainbow of color. They throw colored powder, called gulal, and spray colored water at each other. In the evening, people visit and exchange treats.

Holi Treats

Holi is a joyous holiday celebrated in India. It is a festival that welcomes spring with an explosion of color, singing, dancing, and tasty food. For the holiday, people prepare many kinds of treats to share with their friends and family. Everyone looks forward to sweet round laddu balls made from flour, sugary syrup, nuts, and seeds. Sweet dumplings, called gujiya, and sugary pancake-like deserts, called malpua, are also popular. Thandai is a refreshing cold drink made with milk, nuts, and spices that is enjoyed on Holi.

Continued ➤

SKILL: Compare and Contrast

1. What is Holi?   ⃝ All About Holi   ⃝ Holi Treats   ⃝ both

_____

2. Where is Holi celebrated?   ⃝ All About Holi   ⃝ Holi Treats   ⃝ both

_____

3. What kind of food is eaten on Holi?   ⃝ All About Holi   ⃝ Holi Treats   ⃝ both

_____

4. What is gulal?   ⃝ All About Holi   ⃝ Holi Treats   ⃝ both

_____

5. When is Holi celebrated?   ⃝ All About Holi   ⃝ Holi Treats   ⃝ both

_____

Holi   Same   Holi Treats

_____   _____

_____   _____

Different   Different

SKILL: Compare and Contrast

43. Pets for Children

An author's opinion is their **point of view**. It is how they think and feel.
➥ READ the author's opinion. COLOR the bubble that answers the question.

Every child should have a pet. It is fun to play or cuddle with a pet.
Taking care of a pet teaches children to be responsible. If you can't
own a pet, your child could help care for a friend or neighbor's pet. Pets
need food, water, a safe place to live, and lots of love. This sounds easy,
but sometimes it is a lot of work! You might not want to walk your dog in
the rain or clean up after your pet, but your pet depends on you. Being
dependable is an important skill for children to have. Children will be
rewarded because their pet will grow more and more attached to them
as they care for them. This is a special friendship to have!

1. Does the author feel that every child should have a pet to care for?
   O yes   O no

2. Does the author think that having a pet is fun?
   O yes   O no

3. Does the author think that caring for a pet is always easy?
   O yes   O no

4. Does the author feel that being dependable will help a caregiver have a
   good relationship with their pet?
   O yes   O no

5. Does the author think that children who can't own a pet can still find a
   way to care for a pet?
   O yes   O no

SKILL: Author's View

44. Kangaroos

Good readers look for similarities and differences between information found in different sources.

➡ READ each passage. READ each sentence below. Place a ✓ in the column to show where you could find the information.

Baby Joey

Kangaroos are marsupials. Marsupials are animals that carry their young in pouches. A baby kangaroo is called a joey. When it is born, a joey is not much bigger than a peanut! Right after birth, the tiny joey crawls through its mother's thick fur to the safety of her pouch. Here, the joey will feed and grow until it is old enough to start exploring the world. At first, the joey will come out for short periods of time to learn how to jump and eat plants. When it is about ten months old, the young kangaroo will be ready to live on its own.

All About Kangaroos

Boing, boing, boing! Kangaroos are great jumpers! Large, powerful hind legs allow them to leap 30 feet in one hop. They use their long tails for balance and can reach speeds of over 30 miles an hour. Kangaroos are good swimmers, but they can't walk backward! These interesting animals live in groups, called "mobs," and can be found in Australia and New Guinea. Mother kangaroos carry their babies, called joeys, in a special pouch. Kangaroos are herbivores, which means they eat plants.

	Baby Joey	All About Kangaroos	Both
1. A baby kangaroo is called a joey.			
2. Kangaroos are marsupials.			
3. Kangaroos live in Australia.			
4. Mother kangaroos carry their babies in a pouch.			
5. Kangaroos are good jumpers.			
6. Kangaroos can't walk backward.			

SKILL: Compare and Contrast

45. Slow and Steady

There can be more than one version of the same story.

➡ READ each story. Compare and contrast the two versions to show if the parts are the **same** or **different**. CIRCLE your answer.

Tortoise and Hare

One fine day, Tortoise strolled down a path. Hare zipped by, calling, "Hey there, slowpoke, you'll never get where you're going at that rate!"

"That's OK," replied Tortoise, "I am just enjoying this lovely day. Would you like to join me?"

"You are too slow for me!" mocked Hare.

"Maybe we could have a race," suggested Tortoise.

Hare laughed, and sprinted down the path. After a while, Hare looked back and couldn't even see Tortoise. He stopped for a snack and took a nap. Slowly and steadily, Tortoise moved forward, right past sleeping Hare! Hare woke up just in time to see Tortoise cross the finish line! Tortoise looked back and called, "Slow and steady wins the race!"

Sloth and Jaguar

One morning, Sloth was lazily enjoying the sunshine. Jaguar came along and said, "You must be the slowest creature on earth!" Sloth didn't mind. He didn't have anywhere to go, so it didn't matter how long it took to get there.

"Would you like to watch the sunlight with me?" he invited Jaguar.

"Too boring for me!" replied Jaguar.

"Perhaps you would like to race to the sun," suggested Sloth.

"Game on!" cried Jaguar speeding upward. Eventually, he looked down and couldn't see Sloth anywhere. He decided to take a nap. Vine after vine, Sloth gradually pulled himself upward. Up, up, up he went, right past sleeping Jaguar! Jaguar woke up just in time to see Sloth reach the treetops. Looking backward, Sloth shouted, "Slow and steady wins the race!"

1. Characters   **same**   **different**
2. Setting   **same**   **different**
3. Problem   **same**   **different**
4. Ending   **same**   **different**
5. Lesson   **same**   **different**

SKILL: Compare and Contrast

PART 2

Writing

1. A Litter of Puppies

A **collective noun** names a group of people, animals, or things. There are many words that mean "group" in the English language. **Bunch**, **batch**, and **flock** are some of the words used to name a group of nouns. A group of puppies is a litter!

➡ READ the words in the box. FILL IN the word from the box that best completes each sentence.

> batch   team   bunch   pair   stack   dozen   flock   pack   band
> collection   bouquet   class

1. We bought a _____ eggs at the farm stand.
2. My sister gave me a _____ of gum.
3. Dad bought a _____ of bananas at the store.
4. Her basketball _____ won the championship!
5. The _____ of musicians will march in the parade.
6. I picked a _____ of flowers for my mother.
7. The _____ of students will visit the museum.
8. A _____ of birds flew right over my head!
9. My grandfather baked a _____ of cookies.
10. There is a _____ of wood behind the shed.
11. Mr. Li has a large _____ of seashells.
12. Mia has a new _____ of sneakers.

2. A Gaggle of Geese

When there is a group of animals together, the group has a special name. The name is a **collective noun**. Some of these names may be familiar, like a **school** of fish. Other times the names are strange or funny, such as a **gaggle** of geese!

➡ UNSCRAMBLE the letters to learn the collective noun for each group of animals. WRITE the word in the blank space. Use the word bank in the box below as a reference.

> flock   wisdom   nest   colony   swarm   school   lounge   band
> crash   prickle   scurry   family   sloth   caravan   pod   pack
> mob   pride   zeal   litter

1. dop   a _____ of whales
2. reipd   a _____ of lions
3. cpka   a _____ of wolves
4. yoocnl   a _____ of bats
5. ncaaavr   a _____ of camels
6. ttleri   a _____ of kittens
7. wsamr   a _____ of bees
8. omb   a _____ of kangaroos
9. ckflo   a _____ of sheep
10. sten   a _____ of mice
11. chloos   a _____ of dolphins
12. ascrh   a _____ of rhinoceros
13. usrcry   a _____ of squirrels
14. mifayl   a _____ of beavers
15. thols   a _____ of bears
16. nabd   a _____ of gorillas
17. clekrip   a _____ of porcupines
18. siwmod   a _____ of wombats
19. ezal   a _____ of zebras
20. ounlge   a _____ of lizards

SKILL: Nouns

3. Making More

When there is more than one person, place, or thing, you usually add **-s** or **-es** to the end of the noun to make a **plural noun**. However, that doesn't work every time. Some plural nouns are **irregular** and don't follow the rules. For example, the plural of **mouse** is **mice**. These exceptions to the rules will get easier to remember with practice!

➡ COLOR the bubble next to the correct plural noun that completes the sentence. WRITE the word on the line.

1. My hungry brother ate three _____ for lunch.
   ○ sandwichs   ○ sandwich   ○ sandwiches

2. Mr. Rodriguez has pretty _____ growing in his garden.
   ○ flowers   ○ flower   ○ floweres

3. The _____ are running in a road race.
   ○ woman   ○ womans   ○ women

4. The _____ are flying south for the winter.
   ○ gooses   ○ goose   ○ geese

5. The _____ are eating clover in the field.
   ○ cowes   ○ cows   ○ cow

6. I counted 12 _____ in that tree!
   ○ birds   ○ bird   ○ birdes

7. We need a lot of _____ to make spaghetti sauce.
   ○ tomatos   ○ tomato   ○ tomatoes

8. I can hear the _____ howling at the moon.
   ○ wolfs   ○ wolves   ○ wolfes

9. My brother and I will help wash the _____ after dinner.
   ○ dishes   ○ dishs   ○ dishess

10. The hikers saw three _____ on their camping trip.
    ○ mooses   ○ moos   ○ moose

4. Rule Breakers

To make a **plural noun**, you usually add **-s** or **-es** to the end of a noun. This shows that there is more than one person, place, or thing. Some plural nouns break the rules. They are called **irregular plural nouns**. For example, the plural of **goose** is **geese**. These exceptions to the rules will get easier to remember with practice!

➡ DRAW a line to connect each noun and each picture to its matching irregular plural noun.

foot	mice
	children
child	oxen
	leaves
man	deer
	fish
scarf	feet
	scarves
ox	teeth
	men
person	moose
	people

SKILL: Nouns

5. Test Your Reflexes

Reflexive pronouns are pronouns that refer back to the subject of a sentence. Reflexive pronouns end with **-self** or **-selves**. Here is an example of a reflexive pronoun used in a sentence:

Katya hurt (herself) when she was cutting carrots.

The reflexive pronoun *herself* refers back to the subject, *Katya*.

➡ CIRCLE the **reflexive pronoun** in each sentence. DRAW a line under the **subject**.

1. Peter washed the car all by himself.

2. The children are playing by themselves in the sandbox.

3. We built our house ourselves.

4. I can climb the stairs myself.

5. You may help yourself to some cookies.

6. Julie and I enjoyed ourselves at the movies.

7. The bird built itself a nest.

8. She built a robot for the science fair by herself.

9. I can tie my shoes all by myself.

10. My sister sang a song by herself in the school play.

11. They used the key to let themselves into the gym.

12. The dragon flew itself to a magical kingdom.

SKILL: Nouns

6. Reflexology

Reflexive pronouns end in **-self** or **-selves**. They refer back to the subject of the sentence.

➡ COLOR the bubble next to the word that best completes each sentence. WRITE the word on the line.

1. The girl saw _____ in the mirror.
   ○ herself   ○ itself   ○ themselves

2. I can brush my hair by _____.
   ○ ourselves   ○ myself   ○ itself

3. We went to the store by _____.
   ○ herself   ○ itself   ○ ourselves

4. They helped _____ to the cookies.
   ○ themselves   ○ ourselves   ○ itself

5. He can't fix the car by _____.
   ○ myself   ○ itself   ○ himself

6. The beaver built a house out of sticks by _____.
   ○ herself   ○ itself   ○ themselves

7. Can you finish the chores by _____?
   ○ yourself   ○ itself   ○ herself

BONUS! What can you do all by yourself? Write three sentences below.
Use the word **myself** in each sentence.

1. _____

2. _____

3. _____

SKILL: Nouns

7. Now and Then

Walk, dance, jump! These words show action. An action word is called a **verb**. A **past tense verb** is used when the action has already happened, like in this sentence:

Yesterday, I **walked** to the store.

Usually, **-ed** or **-d** is added to the end of a verb to turn it into the past tense. Some verbs don't follow the pattern. They are **irregular past tense verbs**.

Here are some verbs with their past tense:

Regular Past Tense Verbs	Irregular Past Tense Verbs
bake—baked	sit—sat
walk—walked	tell—told

➡ COLOR the verb pair **red** if the pattern is regular. COLOR the verb pair **blue** if the pattern is irregular. Three in a row is tic-tac-toe!

walk—walked	hit—hit	cook—cooked		fly—flew	build—built	paint—painted
love—loved	wash—washed	eat—ate		listen—listened	dance—danced	sleep—slept
wish—wished	live—lived	catch—caught		sit—sat	run—ran	tell—told

8. Past and Present

Action words are called **verbs**. **Past tense verbs** are action words that have already happened. To turn a verb into the past tense, you usually add **-d** or **-ed** to the end of the word. **Irregular verbs** don't follow this pattern.

➧ READ each word. DRAW a line to connect the verb to its past tense.

Present Tense Verb	Past Tense Verb
write	sat
go	taught
sit	began
run	wrote
eat	brought
teach	slept
fly	found
hit	gave
bring	came
sleep	ran
begin	ate
find	went
write	broke
come	met
feel	had
break	said
have	wrote
give	hit
meet	flew
say	felt

SKILL: Verbs

9. Describing Words

An **adjective** is a word that describes a noun or pronoun. Adjectives answer questions, such as *How many? What kind? Which one?* An **adverb** describes a verb, adjective, or another adverb. Adverbs answer questions such as *Where? When? How?* They also tell us how likely something will happen. Adverbs usually end in *-ly*.

➡ READ each sentence. WRITE the noun and the adjective that describes the noun on the lines.

	Noun	Adjective
The soft kitten spilled her milk.	_____	_____
The muddy pig is eating its dinner.	_____	_____
Many chickens are in the yard.	_____	_____
That is a beautiful rainbow.	_____	_____
The spotted cow is my favorite.	_____	_____

➡ READ each sentence. WRITE the verb and the adverb that describes the verb in the boxes.

	Verb	Adverb
The farmer sells vegetables weekly.	_____	_____
The rooster crows noisily.	_____	_____
The horse quickly runs across the field.	_____	_____
The farmer carefully milks the cow.	_____	_____
The bunny will likely win a prize at the county fair.	_____	_____

SKILL: Adjectives and Adverbs

10. Adjective or Adverb?

Adjectives describe nouns. They tell us how many, what kind, and which.
Adverbs describe verbs, adjectives, and other adverbs. They tell us where, when, and how.

➡ READ each sentence. COLOR the bubble to show whether the word in **bold** is an adjective or an adverb.

1. The stars shine **brightly** in the night sky. ⭕ adjective ⭕ adverb

2. My sister is the **smallest** one in the family. ⭕ adjective ⭕ adverb

3. The **tall** giraffe can reach the leaves in the tree. ⭕ adjective ⭕ adverb

4. The athlete trains **daily** for the marathon. ⭕ adjective ⭕ adverb

5. His dog is sleeping **peacefully** under the table. ⭕ adjective ⭕ adverb

6. The **fluffy** chicks are hungry. ⭕ adjective ⭕ adverb

7. The drummer bangs the drums **loudly**. ⭕ adjective ⭕ adverb

8. My uncle makes **delicious** tacos. ⭕ adjective ⭕ adverb

9. We are planning a **surprise** party for Maria. ⭕ adjective ⭕ adverb

10. The monkey can climb the tree **easily**. ⭕ adjective ⭕ adverb

11. I **always** eat my vegetables. ⭕ adjective ⭕ adverb

12. The little boy is whispering **quietly**. ⭕ adjective ⭕ adverb

SKILL: Adjectives and Adverbs

11. Paint a Picture!

A **simple sentence** contains a subject and a verb. It doesn't tell the reader very much.

The mouse ate a strawberry.

Did you picture a white mouse or a gray one? Was the strawberry sweet, mushy, juicy, or red? We don't really know. When writers describe nouns with sensory words, it helps the reader imagine how something looks, sounds, feels, smells, or tastes. These adjectives paint a picture in the reader's imagination!

➡ READ the sentences. LOOK at the pictures. Make the sentence more descriptive by adding an adjective before each noun. Then, color the pictures to match your descriptions.

1. The _____ **dinosaur** ran away from the _____ **volcano**.

2. The _____ **bear** is making a _____ **pizza**.

3. The _____ **monkey** is eating a _____ **banana**.

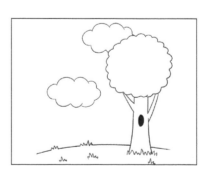

4. The _____ **cloud** is in the _____ **sky**.

SKILL: Sentence Structure

12. Build a Better Sentence

A **simple sentence** contains a subject and a verb. Adjectives and adverbs can be added to a simple sentence to make it more descriptive.

Here is a simple sentence: My dog barks.

Let's try adding an adjective: My **little** dog barks.

Now let's try adding an adverb: My little dog barks **loudly**.

Writers use **expanded sentences** to tell a vivid story.

➡ READ the words in each box. WRITE an adjective on the blue line and an adverb on the red line in each expanded sentence below.

Adjectives

> cute, bright, sticky, strange, happy, silly, talented, joyful, little, juicy, sweet, serious, messy, shiny, new, old, stupid, happy, sad, large, small

Adverbs

> quietly, skillfully, loudly, quickly, brightly, lovingly, hungrily, noisily, sloppily, beautifully, radiantly, tomorrow, yesterday, frequently, often, sweetly

1. The _____ cat played _____.

2. He _____ strummed his _____ guitar.

3. My _____ sister is eating _____.

4. Carlos ate some _____ grapes _____.

5. The _____ sun is shining _____.

SKILL: Sentence Structure

13. Scrambled Eggs for Breakfast

A sentence can make a statement, ask a question, make a command, or show a strong feeling. Sentences begin with a capital letter and end with a punctuation mark.

•

Telling or Command Sentence

!

Strong Feeling Sentence

?

Asking Sentence

➡ UNSCRAMBLE the words and WRITE a statement sentence. Rearrange the words to WRITE a question.

1. scrambled | breakfast | Jose | make | will | eggs | for

   Statement: _____

   Question: _____

2. coffee | can | some | make | Dad

   Statement: _____

   Question: _____

3. some | will | Mom | bacon | crispy | make

   Statement: _____

   Question: _____

4. her | Mia | toast | jam | on | would | like

   Statement: _____

   Question: _____

5. juice | Cory | orange | should | the | pour

   Statement: _____

   Question: _____

SKILL: Sentence Structure

14. Joining Together

A **simple sentence** is also called an **independent clause**. Two independent clauses can be joined together to make a **compound sentence** by using a **conjunction**. *And, or, but*, and *so* are some commonly used conjunctions.

➥ READ the compound sentences. COLOR the *two* circles that show which two simple sentences were combined to make the compound sentence.

1. Airi walks her dog and feeds her cat.
   - ◯ Airi walks her dog and cat.
   - ◯ Airi walks her dog.
   - ◯ Airi feeds her cat.
   - ◯ Airi takes care of her dog and cat.

2. Edward likes to play golf, but he does not like to play tennis.
   - ◯ Edward likes to play golf.
   - ◯ Edward likes to play tennis.
   - ◯ He does not like to play tennis.
   - ◯ Edward likes to play golf and tennis.

3. Learning to ride a bike is difficult, but it is so much fun once you learn!
   - ◯ It is fun to ride a bike!
   - ◯ Riding a bike is difficult but fun.
   - ◯ It is so much fun once you learn!
   - ◯ Learning to ride a bike is difficult.

4. I will practice shooting baskets so I can help my team win the game.
   - ◯ I will play basketball.
   - ◯ I will practice shooting baskets.
   - ◯ I can help my team win the game.
   - ◯ Shooting baskets takes practice.

5. I have to feed my dog, or he will be hungry.
   - ◯ My dog is hungry.
   - ◯ I am going to feed my dog.
   - ◯ I have to feed my dog.
   - ◯ He will be hungry.

SKILL: Sentence Structure

15. Very Proper

A **proper noun** is a noun that names a specific person, place, or thing. No matter where a proper noun is located in a sentence, it begins with a capital letter.

➡ Some of the words in the puzzle should begin with a capital letter. REWRITE the word in the box using capital letters if it is a **proper noun**. COLOR the boxes with a regular noun **blue**. If it is a proper noun, COLOR the box **red**. Three in a row is tic-tac-toe!

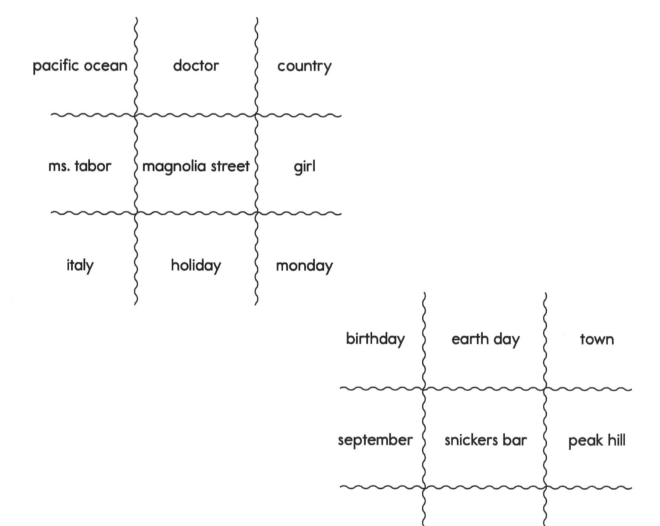

16. Visiting the Capital

Proper nouns name a specific person, place, or thing and begin with a capital letter. Holidays, product names, a person's name, days of the week, months, and specific places are all **proper nouns**.

➡ READ the story. CIRCLE the letters that should be capitalized.

The morez family is going on a trip to washington, DC.

Their plane is leaving on the first saturday in april. They are

going to the national cherry blossom festival. The beautiful

pink trees were a gift from japan. They will see a parade,

hear the jazzy trio play at the kennedy center, and visit the

washington monument. On monday, they will take a super

speedy scooter tour of the city. On tuesday, they will visit the

lincoln memorial, where martin luther king jr. gave his famous

speech. On wednesday, they will have lunch at the capital

burger restaurant with aunt maria. She will take them to see the

national air and space museum in the afternoon. on thursday,

they will visit the smithsonian national museum of american

history. on friday, they will have to fly home to boston. Before

they go to the airport, they will take a family picture in front of

the united states capitol building to remember the fun time they

had on their vacation.

SKILL: Capitalization

17. Lists and Letters

Have you ever seen a comma when you were reading? It looks like this: ,

Commas can be used when listing things. They are also used to separate the day from the year when you write the date. When you write a letter, a comma is used after the greeting and after the closing. Here are some examples:

January 4, 2021   Dear Mayor,   Fondly,
I like peas, carrots, and beans.

➡ LOOK at the punctuation. If it is correct, put a ✓ in the box. If it is incorrect, WRITE it correctly on the line.

1. ☐ March, 10 2008 _____

2. ☐ My dog likes to play with balls, Frisbees and sticks. _____

3. ☐ Fondly, Ms. Topaz _____

4. ☐ Dear Dr. Ali, _____

5. ☐ Sincerely Georgia _____

6. ☐ We are going on a trip to Maine, Vermont, and New Hampshire.
_____

7. ☐ Simone is good at lacrosse basketball and soccer. _____

8. ☐ Dear Ms. Quigley _____

SKILL: Comma Usage

18. Three Wishes

A letter that you write to someone has five parts: the **heading** (date), **greeting**, **body**, **closing**, and **signature**. Commas are always used in the date, the greeting, and the closing. They are sometimes used in the body.

➡ In fairy tales, fairy godmothers and genies often grant three wishes. WRITE about what you would like if you had three wishes. Don't forget to add commas!

_____
                    date

Dear _____
       greeting

I have heard that you can grant wishes! The three things I wish

for are _____

_____ and _____.

I would like the first wish because _____.

The second wish would help me because _____.

The third wish would make me happy because _____.
               body

I hope you will consider granting my wishes!

_____
   closing

_____
   signature

SKILL: Comma Usage

19. On Vacation

A **contraction** is a shorter way to say or write two words. When the words join together, some of the letters in the second word are taken out and replaced by an **apostrophe**. An apostrophe looks like a comma, but it is in the air like this: '

➡ READ the sentence. Replace the words in **blue** with a contraction from the box. WRITE the correct word on the line.

> I've   she'd   we're   hasn't   we'd   couldn't   you're   don't   they'll
> I'm   let's   they're

1. (**I have**) _____ never been to the Grand Canyon, but I hope to go soon!

2. Next week, (**they are**) _____ going on a vacation to Yosemite National Park.

3. I hope you (**do not**) _____ forget to bring your camera!

4. Margo (**has not**) _____ ever been on an airplane.

5. Someday, (**we would**) _____ love to visit the California coast.

6. (**I am**) _____ excited to learn how to ski this winter.

7. After we eat lunch, (**let us**) _____ go on a hike to the waterfall.

8. I think (**she would**) _____ rather go surfing than snowboarding.

9. We (**could not**) _____ go to the amusement park because it was raining.

10. I've noticed that (**you are**) _____ always up for an adventure!

11. This summer, (**they will**) _____ go to a rodeo.

SKILL: Apostrophe Usage

20. Whose Shoes?

A **possessive noun** is a noun that owns something. To show ownership, add **apostrophe + s ('s)** to the end of a singular noun:

> The boy**'s** dog will not bite you.

If a plural noun already ends in **s**, just add the apostrophe:

> The twins**'** birthday is in January.

If a plural noun doesn't end in s, add **apostrophe + s**:

> The children**'s** garden is blooming.

➡ DRAW a line to connect the words to the matching **possessive noun**.

the shoes of my friend	the children's playground
the garden of Mr. Batistini	the bees' hive
the toys of the twins	the tree's apples
the apples of the tree	my friend's shoes
the food of the kitten	the girls' parents
the hive of the bees	Jake's game
the cave of the dragon	Dr. McMahon's car
the football team of the boy	Winny's book
the car of Dr. McMahon	the kitten's food
the playground of the children	the twins' toys
the father of Miguel	the dragon's cave
the game of Jake	Mr. Batistini's garden
the book of Winny	the carpenters' tools
the tools of the carpenters	the boy's football team
the parents of the girls	Miguel's father

SKILL: Apostrophe Usage

21. Turtle Dance

Game, pie, table . . . Did you hear the **e** in those words? Of course not. That's because the **e** was silent. Silent **e** has quite a few jobs to do. Here are some of them:

1 Silent **e** makes the vowel before itself say its name in words that end with vowel-consonant-silent **e**.

kite   made   rope

2 The letters **c** and **g** have a soft sound when they come before a silent **e**.

race   cage

3 Silent **e** donates a vowel sound to the end of syllable-consonant-**l** words because every syllable needs a vowel.

marble   sprinkle   turtle

4 Silent **e** offers to go last so that **i, u, v**, and **z** don't have to.

breeze   forgive   pie

5 Silent **e** can go after the letter **s** in some words to show that the word is not plural.

tease   please   tense

➡ READ each word. COLOR each section using the color in the key on page 68 that matches the silent e rule.

1: grape, cake, kite, bike, rope, nose, flute, cube, plane, dime, hole, rule

2: dance, prance, chance, glance, range, cent, change, gentle, celebrate, cereal, recess

3: middle, simple, sparkle, sizzle, whistle, bubble, giggle, bicycle

4: give, forgive, pie, true, glue, blue, clue, live, tie

5: dense, lapse, mouse, house, tense, goose, moose

SKILL: Spelling Patterns: Silent Letters

22. Keeping Quiet

Silent letters can't be heard when you say the word. The **b** in **comb**, the **d** in **badge**, and the **g** in **sign** are silent letters.

➡ UNSCRAMBLE the letters to write the word. The **bold** letter is silent.

1. nroi**h**   __ h __ __ __

2. geba**d**   __ __ d __ __

3. ssorss**c**i   __ c __ __ __ __ __

4. eraht**w**   w __ __ __ __ __

5. **w**ot   __ w __

6. s**i**ndla   __ s __ __ __

7. **h**wela   __ h __ __ __

8. letsac   __ __ __ t __ __

9. m**b**la   __ __ __ b

10. otk**n**   k __ __ __

11. tleshi**w**   __ h __ __ __ __ __

12. ac**l**kh   __ __ __ l __

SKILL: Spelling Patterns: Silent Letters

23. *R* Is for *Ruler*

In a syllable that has at least one vowel followed by the letter *r*, the **r** is "in charge." The *r* takes over and makes the vowel have a new sound. Can you hear the difference between the **a** in **cat** and the **a** in **car**?

➡ READ the **bold** words. CIRCLE the word in each row that has a *different* vowel sound.

1. **barn**   shark   art   ran   farm

2. **fern**   her   serve   tear   germ

3. **bird**   skirt   rip   chirp   birth

4. **sport**   short   port   road   horn

5. **burn**   turn   trim   surf   curl

6. **arm**   yarn   card   made   part

7. **verse**   merge   term   stern   read

8. **third**   his   girl   dirt   twirl

9. **more**   north   rush   torn   storm

10. **church**   splurge   hurt   cut   curb

SKILL: Spelling Patterns: *r*-Controlled

24. Double Trouble

Sometimes consonants are doubled when adding a suffix, but it's hard to know when. This rule will help:

1 + 1 + 1 Rule

If a word has **1** syllable, **1** vowel, *and* **1** final consonant, then double the final consonant before adding a suffix that starts with a vowel (-*ed*, -*ing*, -*er*, and -*est*). The word **hop** has 1 syllable, 1 vowel (**o**), and 1 final consonant (**p**).

To add a suffix that begins with a vowel, the final consonant needs to be doubled as in **hopped** and **hopping**. Here are some more examples:

big ⟶ bigger, biggest

skip ⟶ skipped, skipping

➡ READ the word. CHECK to see if it matches the **1+1+1 rule**. ADD the suffix. WRITE the new word.

Root Word	One Syllable?	One Vowel?	One Final Consonant?	Add the Suffix	Write the New Word
run	√	√	√	ing	running
help				er	
jump				ing	
trip				ed	
shop				ing	
thin				est	
swim				er	
build				ing	
sleep				ing	
clap				ed	
fast				est	
hug				ing	

SKILL: Spelling Patterns: Suffixes

25. Truck Stop

A **consonant blend** is two or more consonants joined together that each keep their own sound. A blend can come at the beginning or end of a word. The *sn* in *snap* and the *str* in *straw* are consonant blends. A **consonant digraph** is two or more consonants joined together that make a new sound. The *ng* in *wing* and the *ch* in *child* are consonant digraphs.

➽ COLOR the box **red** if the word has a **consonant blend**. Color the box **blue** if it has a **consonant digraph**. Three in a row is tic-tac-toe!

she	think	snow
straw	blow	claw
pretty	why	chocolate

sweep	church	wheel
phone	shoe	spoil
freeze	king	snap

SKILL: Spelling Patterns: Consonant Blends and Digraphs

26. What Do You Hear Here?

Homophones are two or more words that sound the same but have different meanings and spellings.

Here and *hear* are homophones.

Please put your dishes over **here**.

Do you **hear** the bells?

The words sound the same, but they have different spellings and meanings.

➡ READ each sentence. WRITE the correct **homophone** on the line to complete the sentence.

1. Lilacs and daffodils have beautiful (cents/scents/sents) _____.

2. I am making stuffed animals to (cell/sell) _____ at the craft fair.

3. Theo thinks that a (bear/bare) _____ is the most interesting animal.

4. The recipe calls for three cups of (flower/flour) _____.

5. (Hour/Our) _____ family is going on a vacation to Jamaica.

6. Charlie hurt his (right/write) _____ ankle playing basketball.

7. The clothing store is having a (sale/sail) _____ starting on Monday.

8. The dog twitched his (tale/tail) _____ when he saw the squirrel.

9. How long will we have to (weight/wait) _____ in line?

10. Can we come to the park, (to/two/too) _____?

11. She was excited when she (one/won) _____ the race!

12. The (night/knight) _____ in shining armor rode off into the (night/knight) _____.

27. Teaming Up

Vowel teams are two vowels joined together. When two vowels join together, they make a new sound. Sometimes they make the long sound of the first vowel. Other times, they make their own special sound. Remembering which one is which will help you spell them correctly when you write.

➡ READ each word. UNDERLINE the vowel team. WRITE the word in the box that shows the vowel sound.

house	float	coin	cloud	feet	play	beach	train	say	boat
pie	toe	blue	moon	boil	pain	teach	pool	mouse	dream

Long Vowel Sound	Special Sound

SKILL: Spelling Patterns: Vowel Teams

28. Hey, How's It Going?

Have you ever noticed that different language is used depending on the situation? **Informal language** is casual. **Formal language** is the proper way to speak and write. How you speak or write should fit the situation.

➡ WRITE whether you would use **formal** or **informal** language in each situation or activity.

1. at a friend's party

   _____

2. a report about frogs

   _____

3. writing a text message

   _____

4. writing a letter to the mayor

   _____

5. writing a shopping list for yourself

   _____

6. speaking with a police officer

   _____

7. giving a speech

   _____

8. ordering at a restaurant

   _____

➡ READ the informal sentences. REWRITE the sentence to show formal language.

1. What are we **gonna** do after dinner?

   _____

2. **Thanks** for the present.

   _____

3. How **y'all** doing today?

   _____

4. I **gotta** go home now.

   _____

SKILL: Language Usage

29. Baseball Barbecue

You can use clues from a sentence or passage to help you learn new words to use in your own writing.

➡ READ each sentence. COLOR the bubble next to the correct meaning of the words in **bold**.

1. The Bayview Baseball League is having their **annual** barbecue next Saturday. My brother and I look forward to going every year.
   - ⭕ exciting
   - ⭕ delicious
   - ⭕ yearly

2. It is the biggest event in our **community**. Everyone in town is excited to go.
   - ⭕ building
   - ⭕ place where people live
   - ⭕ office

3. Coach Armani asked for **volunteers** to set up tables. My brother and I were happy to help out.
   - ⭕ helpers
   - ⭕ players
   - ⭕ strong people

4. The Bayside Market has offered to **donate** the food. The coach and players are grateful for this generous gift.
   - ⭕ bring
   - ⭕ sell
   - ⭕ give for free

5. Tickets cost 8 dollars a person. The money raised will help **fund** the team trip to the playoffs.
   - ⭕ pay for
   - ⭕ send
   - ⭕ charge money for

6. The weather report **forecasts** rain. The coach is going to set up a tent in case it does.
   - ⭕ makes something happen
   - ⭕ guesses that something might happen
   - ⭕ makes something not happen

7. On the day of the barbecue, the sky is blue and the sun is shining. "We are **fortunate** that the weather is beautiful!" exclaimed the coach.
   - ⭕ lucky
   - ⭕ happy
   - ⭕ having a lot of money

8. The barbecue was a great **success**! The team raised enough money for their trip *and* had some left over to pay for new uniforms.
   - ⭕ challenge
   - ⭕ accomplishment
   - ⭕ event

SKILL: Vocabulary

30. A Piece of Cake

Sometimes words don't say what they mean. An **idiom** is a common expression that has a different meaning than what the words actually say. When something is referred to as "a piece of cake," it means that it is easy to do. We can use clues in the sentence to figure out the meaning of an unknown idiom.

➡ DRAW a line to connect the idioms in **bold** to their meaning.

1. We had to race home because it was **raining cats and dogs**!

2. I was **over the moon** when I won first prize.

3. When Tia lost her keys at the beach, it was **like looking for a needle in a haystack**.

4. Kirsten was **down in the dumps** when her camping trip was cancelled because of rain.

5. My mother said that I could ride my bike without a helmet **when pigs fly**.

6. When I asked dad for a sandwich, he told me to **hold my horses**.

7. When Uncle Leo said he was planning a surprise party for Aunt Clair, he told us not to **let the cat out of the bag**.

8. When the bus left without us, we were **all in the same boat**.

9. When my friend and I splashed in a puddle, our coach told us that we were like **two peas in a pod**.

10. My aunt showed up today **out of the blue**.

a. extremely happy

b. exactly alike

c. sad

d. wait

e. reveal a secret

f. impossible to find

g. raining hard

h. sharing the same problem

i. as a surprise

j. never

SKILL: Vocabulary

31. Know It All

When you know the meaning of a **base word** and a known **prefix** is added
to it, you can figure out the meaning of an unknown word.

➡ UNDERLINE the prefix. WRITE the meaning of the word.

1. unlock = _____

2. mistrust = _____

3. revisit = _____

4. disagree = _____

5. incorrect = _____

6. preschool = _____

7. refill = _____

8. misunderstood = _____

9. unfair = _____

10. redo = _____

SKILL: Prefixes

32. Prefix Practice

A **base word**, sometimes called a **root word**, is a word that can be added onto. When a **prefix** is added to the beginning of a root or base word, you can change the meaning of the word. If you know the meaning of the word *and* the prefix, you can figure out the meaning of the new word.

➠ READ the word and the definition. If the definition is **true**, color the box **blue**. If the definition is **false** (not true), color the box **red**. Three in a row is tic-tac-toe!

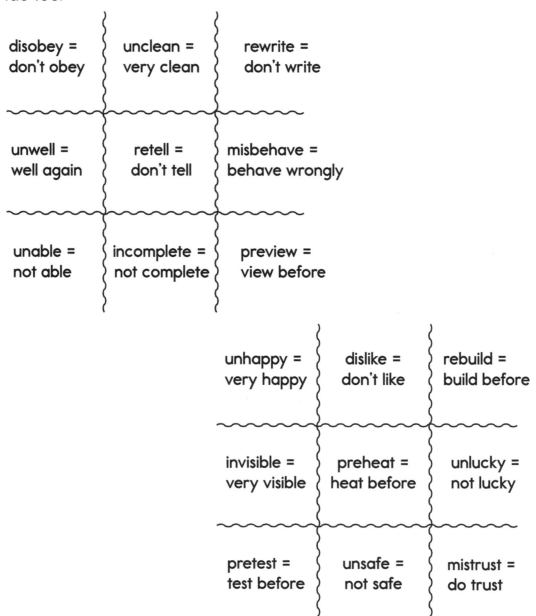

disobey = don't obey	unclean = very clean	rewrite = don't write
unwell = well again	retell = don't tell	misbehave = behave wrongly
unable = not able	incomplete = not complete	preview = view before

unhappy = very happy	dislike = don't like	rebuild = build before
invisible = very visible	preheat = heat before	unlucky = not lucky
pretest = test before	unsafe = not safe	mistrust = do trust

SKILL: Prefixes

33. Add to It!

A **base word**, sometimes called a **root word**, is a word that can be made into new words by adding a prefix or suffix to it. This can help you understand the meaning of a word you don't know.

➡ DRAW a line to connect the word to the meaning of its **base word**.

cheerful	join together
courageous	rule
jewelry	person in a group
youngster	gem
talkative	speak
addition	bravery
government	not old
membership	good mood

SKILL: Root Words

34. Get to the Root of It

A **base word** can help you figure out the meaning of a word you don't know. If you know what the base word means, you have a clue that will help you figure out the meaning of the new word. Let's look at an example:

Word	Base Word	Base Word Meaning
educational	educate	to give knowledge, teach

➡ WRITE the root word and its meaning on the lines.

Word	Base Word	Base Word Meaning
1. actor	_____	_____
2. subtraction	_____	_____
3. unexpectedly	_____	_____
4. spicy	_____	_____
5. doubtful	_____	_____
6. airy	_____	_____
7. behavior	_____	_____
8. unusual	_____	_____
9. unlucky	_____	_____
10. friendship	_____	_____

SKILL: Root Words

35. Word + Word

A **compound word** is two words joined together to make a new word. You can use what you know about each word to predict the meaning of the new word. For example, *cup* + *cake* = *cupcake*.

➡ WRITE the missing part of the compound word. Use the pictures as clues.

1. _____ house

2. snow _____

3. foot _____

4. sun _____

5. butter _____

6. _____ cloth

7. _____ set

8. _____ print

9. pop _____

10. scare _____

36. Word Whiz

A **compound word** is two words added together to make a new word. If you know the meaning of each word, you can predict the meaning of the new word. For example, *star* + *fish* = *starfish*.

➡ CHOOSE a word from the box to make a new word. WRITE the compound word.

glasses, card, boy, coat, ball, place, cut, hole, flake, box

1. sun + _____ = _____

2. sand + _____ = _____

3. post + _____ = _____

4. hair + _____ = _____

5. fire + _____ = _____

6. cow + _____ = _____

7. rain + _____ = _____

8. key + _____ = _____

9. snow + _____ = _____

10. base + _____ = _____

SKILL: Compound Words

37. Good, Great, Awesome!

Adjectives can have similar meanings. Choosing the best one to describe what you are writing about will give the reader a picture in their mind of what something is like. Which sentence gives you a clearer picture in your mind?

> My sister had a **good** idea.
>
> My sister had a **brilliant** idea.

➡ COLOR the bubble next to the *most* descriptive adjective that could be used to describe the noun in the sentence. WRITE the adjective on the line to finish the sentence.

1. The _____ **elephant** stood next to the tiny mouse.
   ○ big   ○ large   ○ humongous

2. We had a _____ **day** at the fair.
   ○ good   ○ fantastic   ○ nice

3. Did you hear the _____ **storm** last night?
   ○ bad   ○ loud   ○ thunderous

4. The ballet dancer wore a _____ **costume**.
   ○ gorgeous   ○ pretty   ○ nice

5. When we got home, our dog had made a(n) _____ **mess**!
   ○ big   ○ enormous   ○ great

6. On a hot day there is nothing like a _____ **lemonade**.
   ○ cold   ○ cool   ○ frosty

7. The _____ **sun** melted my ice cream before I could eat it!
   ○ scorching   ○ hot   ○ warm

8. The field of _____ **daffodils** blooms every spring.
   ○ bright   ○ yellow   ○ golden

9. The _____ **clown** makes everyone laugh.
   ○ funny   ○ hilarious   ○ silly

10. The _____ **buildings** have lasted a very long time.
    ○ ancient   ○ old   ○ aging

SKILL: Word Relationships

38. Burst of Energy

A **verb** describes the action in a sentence. A **common verb** describes the action in a very simple way. A **strong verb** gives the reader a better idea of what the action is like. Which sentence gives you a better picture in your mind of what is happening in the scene described below?

> The fox **ran** after the mouse.
>
> The fox **sprinted** after the mouse.

➡ DRAW a line to connect the **common verb** to the similar **strong verb**.

Common Verbs	Strong Verbs
sleep	slurp
cry	shatter
disappear	snooze
throw	vanish
bother	clutch
ask	hurl
drink	whimper
walk	tiptoe
hold	question
break	annoy

SKILL: Word Relationships

39. Fact vs. Opinion

A **fact** is information that can be proven to be true. An **opinion** is the way someone thinks or feels. It can't be proven to be right or wrong.

➡ READ each sentence. DECIDE if it is a **fact** or an **opinion**. CIRCLE your answer.

1. Canadian geese fly south for the winter.   Fact   Opinion

2. It is scary to watch bats fly through the night.   Fact   Opinion

3. Every child should play a sport.   Fact   Opinion

4. There are seven days in a week.   Fact   Opinion

5. Plants need water and sunshine to grow.   Fact   Opinion

6. Cats make good pets because they are soft and cuddly.   Fact   Opinion

7. The sun is the center of the solar system.   Fact   Opinion

8. Sunflowers are fun to grow in your garden   Fact   Opinion

9. It is easy to learn to play the piano.   Fact   Opinion

10. A piano has eighty-eight keys.   Fact   Opinion

11. A cactus plant stores water in its stems, roots, and leaves.   Fact   Opinion

12. Florida is the best state to live in because it is warm all year. Fact   Opinion

That's just *your* opinion.

BEST PET

SKILL: Opinion Piece

40. The Perfect Pet

An **opinion** is the way someone thinks or feels about something. A **reason** is why they think or feel the way they do. In an **opinion piece**, a writer shares their opinion and give reasons and examples for feeling the way they do.

What kind of animal do you think would be the perfect pet? Why do you think so? FINISH writing the opinion piece below.

In my opinion, the perfect pet is a _____

_____

I think this because _____

_____

I also feel that _____

_____

An example is _____

_____

This is why I think that _____

_____

SKILL: Opinion Piece

41. Getting Organized

In an **opinion piece**, a writer states their opinion, gives reasons and examples for their opinion, and restates their opinion at the end. A **graphic organizer** will help organize your ideas before you write a final draft.

➡ FILL IN the graphic organizer to show how you would plan to write an opinion piece about a book you have read. COLOR the bubble next to the sentence starter in each section that you would like to use. WRITE your ideas on the lines.

My Opinion
In my opinion, I think that
the book _____ by _____
was _____.

Reason 1:
○ First,   ○ To begin with,   ○ To start with,
_____

Reason 2:
○ Another reason   ○ Secondly,   ○ Another reason,
_____

Example:
○ For example,   ○ For instance,   ○ In addition,
_____

Ending:
○ Finally,   ○ As you can see,   ○ In conclusion
_____

SKILL: Opinion Piece

42. You're the Expert

An **informative text** provides the reader with information about a topic. It includes facts, details, examples, and explanations.

➡ Choose one of the topic ideas from the box to write about. FINISH the informative text by providing information about your topic.

pet care   a sport   your town or city   a hobby   a subject   a holiday
(for example, dinosaurs, oceans, volcanoes)

Topic Sentence: _____

Detail 1: _____

_____

Detail 2: _____

_____

Detail 3: _____

_____

Closing: _____

_____

SKILL: Informative Text

43. Polar Bear Information

In an **informative text**, the writer shares information with the reader. How a text is organized is called **text structure**. Here are five common types of text structure:

Description: Describe something.

Sequence: Show the order in which things happened or the steps of a procedure.

Compare and contrast: Tell how two things are the same and different.

Cause and effect: Tell *what* happened and *why*.

Problem and solution: Describe a problem and explain the solution.

➡ DRAW a line to connect the informative writing to its matching text structure.

Polar bears have four legs and a whitish coat.

Baby polar bears are the size of a stick of butter when they are born. In a couple of months they weigh 20 pounds. Adult polar bears can weigh over 1,000 pounds!

Problem and Solution

Sequence

Polar bears and grizzly bears are both big and powerful. Their coats are different colors.

Compare and Contrast

Description

Polar bears live in the icy arctic circle. Climate change is causing arctic ice to melt. Polar bears are part of their habitat each year.

Cause and Effect

Ice is difficult to walk on. Polar bears have grips on the pads of their feet that keep them from slipping.

SKILL: Informative Text

44. Imagine That!

Narrative writing tells a story. **Temporal words** are used to help readers understand when events in the story happened. *One day, first, next, suddenly, finally,* and *last* are examples of temporal words. A narrative can be real or imaginary.

➡ LOOK at the picture. Use your imagination to think of what might have happened before and after the picture. DRAW a picture of what happened before and after. WRITE a narrative.

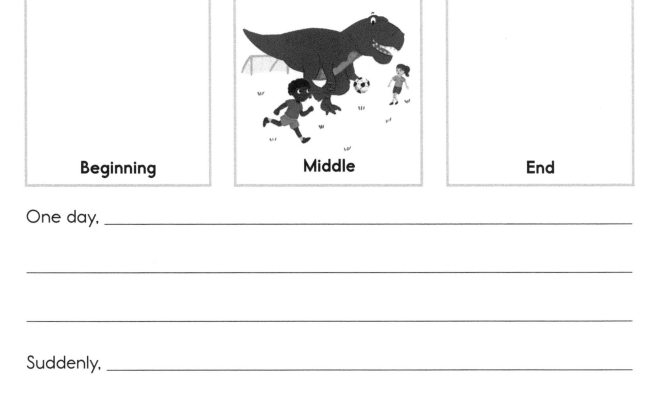

| Beginning | Middle | End |

One day, _____

_____

_____

Suddenly, _____

_____

Finally, _____

_____

_____

SKILL: Narrative

45. Hooray for Me!

A **narrative** is a real or imaginary story told through a sequence of events. Narratives use **temporal words** to tell when something in the story happened.

➡ THINK of a time you tried really hard to do something and succeeded. READ the temporal words in the box. WRITE a story about what you did and how you succeeded. Use one word from each box to tell the order that things happened.

Beginning	**Middle**	**End**
First, One day, One time, In the beginning, To start, It all started when, Once upon a time,	Secondly, Suddenly, Afterward, A while later, After that, Soon, Next, Later, Secondly,	Finally, At last, In the end, Eventually, Lastly, Last, As a result,

I remember a time when I wanted to _____

(Beginning) _____

_____

(Middle) _____

_____

(End) _____

_____

SKILL: Narrative

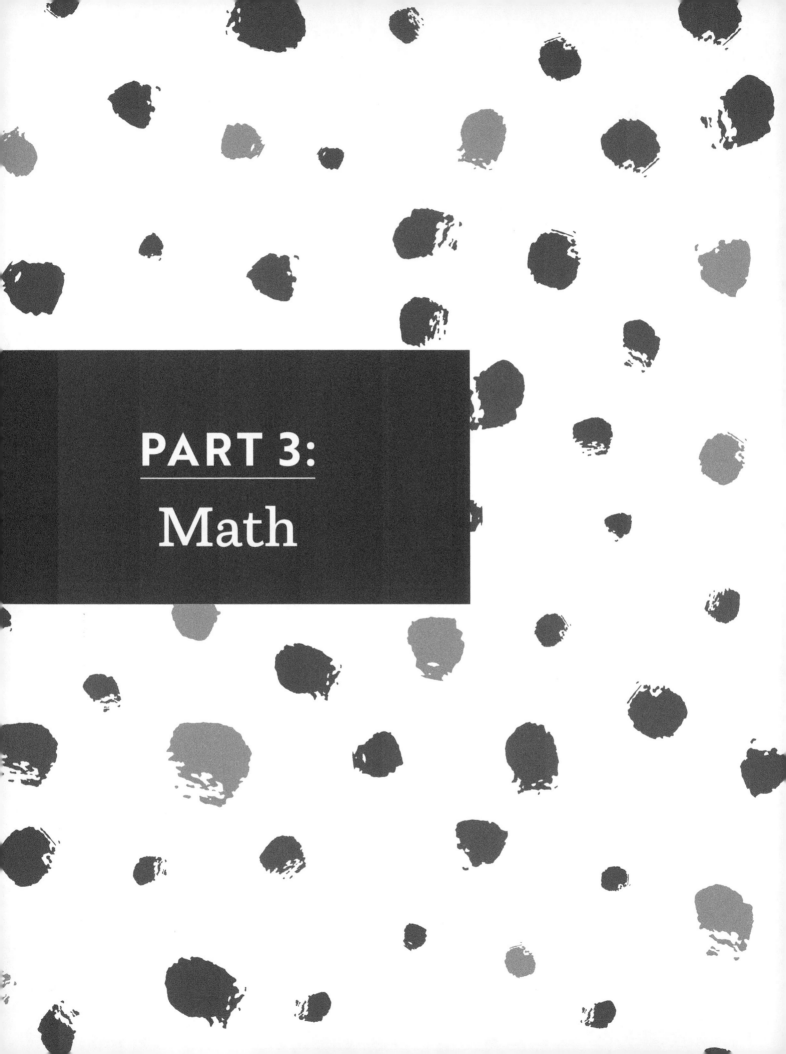

PART 3:
Math

1. Problem Solver

Equations are math sentences that have an **equal sign** (=). You can write and solve math problems by drawing pictures and writing an equation.
➡ READ each problem. On another piece of paper, DRAW a picture or lines for each of the items listed. FINISH the equation by writing the missing numbers on the lines and the missing symbols in the squares.

1. Carlos has a box of 24 crayons. His grandmother gives him another box that has 48 crayons. How many crayons does Carlos have now? ____ + ____ ☐ ____	**2.** Rosa has a box of 60 nails. She uses 48 nails to build a bird house. How many does she have left? ____ ☐ ____ = ____
3. Francisca read 21 books last summer. Ana read 18 books, and Bao read 19 books. How many books did they read altogether? ____ + ____ ☐ ____ = ____	**4.** The library bookmobile has 77 books. It lends out 43 books, and then 15 books are returned. How many books does it have at the end of the day? ____ ☐ ____ + ____ = ____
5. Marcus buys a birthday present for his mother that costs $26. He has $68 left. How much money did he start with? ____ + ____ ☐ ____	**6.** Amal bakes 100 muffins for the family reunion. There are 37 blueberry muffins and 28 lemon muffins. The rest are strawberry. How many strawberry muffins did she bake? 100 ☐ (37 + 28) = ____

SKILL: Word Problems

2. Math in the Forest

An **equation** is a math sentence that is equal on both sides. An **equal sign** (=) separates the two sides.

➡ READ each problem. On another piece of paper, DRAW lines for each item to help you solve it. COLOR the bubble next to the equation that correctly matches the problem.

1. Squirrel is getting ready for the winter. He collects 25 acorns on Monday. On Tuesday, he collects 13, and on Wednesday, he collects 52. How many acorns has he collected?

   ○ 25 + 13 – 52 = 92   ○ 25 + 13 + 52 = 90   ○ 25 + 13 + 52 = 92

2. There are 69 birds in the forest. 27 birds fly south for the winter. How many birds are left?

   ○ 69 + 27 = 96   ○ 69 – 42 = 27   ○ 69 – 27 = 42

3. Bear picks 80 berries to bring home to her cubs. On her way home, she drops 13 berries. She sees another bush and picks 27 more berries. How many berries will she bring home to her cubs?

   ○ 80 – 13 + 27 = 94   ○ 80 + 13 – 27 = 66   ○ 80 + 13 + 27 = 94

4. There are 47 frogs sitting on the lily pads. A loud noise scares 14 frogs and they hop into the water. How many frogs are left on the lily pads?

   ○ 47 + 14 = 61   ○ 47 + 14 = 63   ○ 47 – 14 = 33

5. The forest is blooming with flowers. There are 88 violets and 69 daisies. How many more violets are there than daisies?

   ○ 88 + 69 = 19   ○ 88 – 69 = 19   ○ 19 + 69 = 88

SKILL: Word Problems

3. Family Tree

A **fact family** is a group of math facts that use the same set of numbers.
➡ Each apple has three numbers that make up a fact family. FINISH the
equations using what you know about each of them.

Tree 1 (apples: 7, 15, 8)

7 + ___ = 15

8 + 7 = ___

15 - ___ = 8

___ - 8 = 7

Tree 2 (apples: 6, 11, 5)

___ + 6 = 11

6 + ___ = ___

11 - ___ = 6

___ - 6 = ___

Tree 3 (apples: 7, 9, 2)

___ + ___ = 9

2 + ___ = ___

___ - 7 = ___

___ - ___ = 7

Tree 4 (apples: 11, 20, 9)

___ + 11 = 20

___ + ___ = ___

___ - 9 = ___

20 - ___ = 9

Tree 5 (apples: 9, 17, 8)

___ + ___ = 17

___ + ___ = 17

17 - ___ = 8

17 - ___ = 9

Tree 6 (apples: 4, 7, 3)

___ + 4 = ___

___ + ___ = 7

___ - ___ = 3

7 - ___ = ___

Tree 7 (apples: 6, 14, 8)

___ + ___ = ___

___ + ___ = ___

___ - ___ = ___

___ - ___ = ___

Tree 8 (apples: 8, 11, 3)

___ + ___ = ___

___ + ___ = ___

___ - ___ = ___

___ - ___ = ___

SKILL: Addition and Subtraction

4. Learning to Ride

Learning to ride a bike takes practice, but once you learn, it will seem easy. The same is true for learning **addition** and **subtraction** facts. The more practice you have, the easier it will be!

➡ SOLVE the equations. COLOR each section using the color in the key that matches your answer.

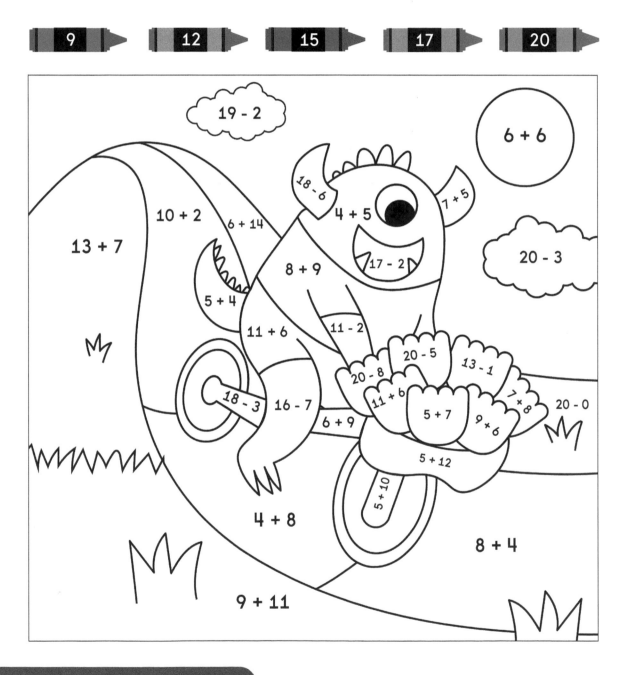

SKILL: Addition and Subtraction

5. A Pair of Pears

Even numbers can be divided into equal parts. **Odd numbers** cannot. An even number can be written as a **doubles addition equation** with equal parts. For example, **8** can be written as **4 + 4 = 8**.

➡ CIRCLE groups of 2. WRITE a doubles addition equation if the number is even.

1.

Is 18 an even number?   yes   no

____ + ____ = _____

2.

Is 16 an even number?   yes   no

____ + ____ = _____

3.

Is 17 an even number?   yes   no

____ + ____ = _____

4.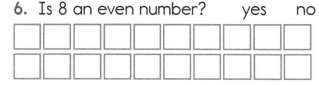

Is 20 an even number?   yes   no

____ + ____ = _____

➡ COLOR the squares in pairs—top and bottom—to show the number given.

5. Is 9 an even number?   yes   no

6. Is 8 an even number?   yes   no

7. Is 15 an even number?   yes   no

8. Is 11 an even number?   yes   no

SKILL: Equal Groups

6. Snack Time

Groups of numbers or objects can be arranged in a grid of columns and rows called an **array**. A **rectangular array** is a group that is arranged in equal rows and columns. Putting objects into an array makes them easier to count and add.

➡ DRAW a line to connect the array to the matching equation.

6 + 6 + 6 = 18

5 + 5 + 5 = 15

4 + 4 + 4 + 4 = 16

3 + 3 + 3 = 9

6 + 6 = 12

5 + 5 + 5 + 5 = 20

SKILL: Equal Groups

7. Sports Store

When objects are placed in an **array**, they are easier to count. A **rectangular array** is a group that can be arranged into equal rows and columns.

➡ WRITE an equation for each **rectangular array**.

1.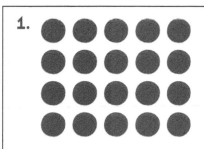

5 + 5 + 5 + 5 = 20

2.

_____

3.

_____

4.

_____

5.

_____

6.

_____

7.

_____

8.

_____

SKILL: Equal Groups

8. Hundreds, Tens, and Ones

Each digit in a number has a **place**, and each place represents an amount (value). The three digits of a three-digit number have values of **hundreds**, **tens**, and **ones**. The number 398 equals 3 hundreds, 9 tens, and 8 ones.

➡ WRITE the number of **hundreds**, **tens**, and **ones** next to each number.

3-Digit Number	How Many hundreds?	How Many Tens?	How Many Ones?
1. 845			
2. 978			
3. 107			
4. 267			
5. 743			
6. 690			
7. 555			
8. 401			
9. 234			
10. 432			

➡ WRITE the number.

11. Write the number that has 6 hundreds, 5 tens, and 0 ones. _____

12. Write the number that has 8 hundreds, 0 tens, and 2 ones. _____

13. Write the number that has 3 hundreds, 3 tens, and 1 one. _____

14. Write the number that has 2 hundreds, 6 tens, and 7 ones. _____

15. Write the number that has 4 hundreds, 6 tens, and 2 ones. _____

SKILL: Place Value

9. Lucky 7

Place value is the value of a digit based on its position in a number. The number 734 equals 7 hundreds, 3 tens, and 4 ones.

Hundreds	Tens	Ones
7	3	4

➡ If the number has a 7 in the hundreds place, COLOR the square **red**. If it does not, COLOR the square **blue**. Three in a row is tic-tac-toe!

799	672	177
237	751	407
771	705	727

➡ If the number has a 7 in the tens place, COLOR the square **orange**. If it does not, COLOR the square **purple**. Three in a row is tic-tac-toe!

347	172	729
977	777	207
751	173	478

➡ If the number has a 7 in the ones place, COLOR the square **green**. If it does not, COLOR the square **yellow**. Three in a row is tic-tac-toe!

707	751	622
197	987	706
347	174	567

SKILL: Place Value

10. Bundle Up!

The number 100 can be shown as 100 single cubes. If you arranged those cubes into a rectangular array, you would have 10 rows of 10 cubes. If you bundled all of the rows and columns together, you would have one bundle of 100 cubes. **Base ten blocks** can be used to show how blocks can be bundled to show tens and hundreds.

➦ COUNT the number of hundreds, tens, and ones. WRITE the amounts on the lines.

1.

_____ hundreds _____ tens _____ ones = _____

2.

_____ hundreds _____ tens _____ ones = _____

3.

_____ hundreds _____ tens _____ ones = _____

4.

_____ hundreds _____ tens _____ ones = _____

SKILL: Number Representation

11. Base Ten Blocks

Base ten blocks represent **place value** and can be used as a tool to solve problems. Two hundreds blocks show us that the number 200 has 2 hundreds. We can also use them to show that 20 tens blocks equal 200 or that 200 ones blocks equal 200.

➡ WRITE the number.

1. 3 hundreds = _____

2. 40 tens = _____

3. 100 ones = _____

4. 8 hundreds = _____

5. 50 tens = _____

6. 300 ones = _____

➡ Look at the base ten blocks. Write the number next to each group.

7. = _____

8. = _____

9. = _____

10. = _____

SKILL: Number Representation

12. Hop, Skip, Jump!

If you counted by ones, it would take a long time to count all the way up to 1000. If you counted by 100s, it would take no time at all! This is called **skip counting**. It is counting while skipping a number or numbers in between. The amount you skip over must be the same every time.

➡ LOOK at the number lines below. WRITE the missing numbers.

1.

0 5 10 15 20   30 35 40 45   55 60 65 70   80 85 90 95 100

2.

0 10 20 30 40 50   70 80 90 100 110 120 130   150 160 170 180   200

3.
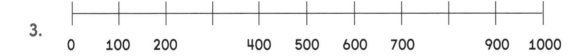

0   100   200   400   500   600   700   900   1000

4.
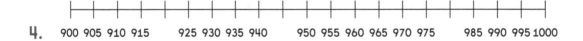

900 905 910 915   925 930 935 940   950 955 960 965 970 975   985 990 995 1000

5.
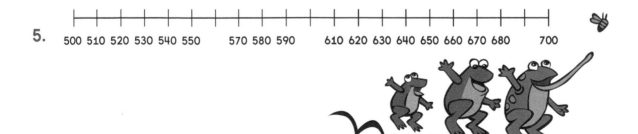

500 510 520 530 540 550   570 580 590   610 620 630 640 650 660 670 680   700

SKILL: Expanded Counting

13. Super Speedy

Skip counting is a faster way to count because you skip numbers in between the ones you count. Just remember to skip over the same amount each time!

➡ FILL IN the number missing from each sequence. COLOR each section using the color key that matches the count-by pattern.

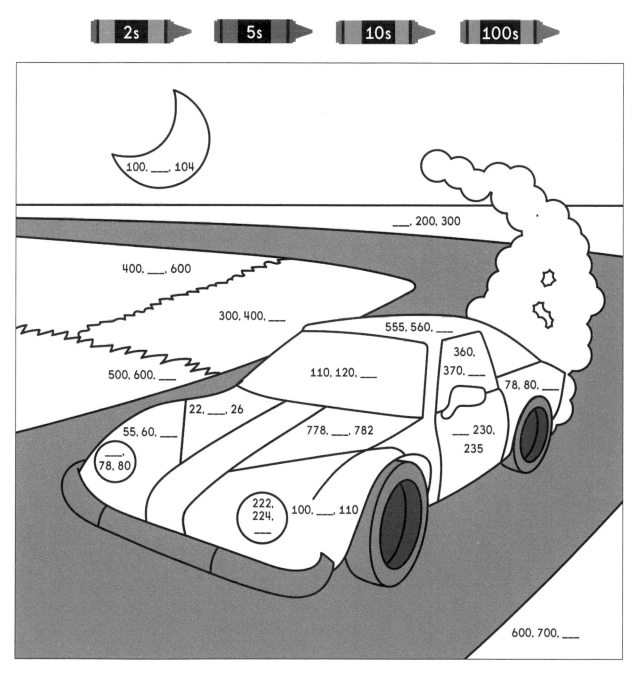

14. Make a Match

Numbers can be written with words and with **numerals**. Three hundred fifty-seven is the same as 357. The number has three hundreds, five tens, and seven ones.

➡ DRAW a line to connect the written number word to the matching numeral.

Seven hundred ninety-nine	645
Three hundred forty-two	561
Six hundred forty-five	799
Four hundred three	814
Nine hundred twenty-four	222
Five hundred sixty-one	403
Eight hundred fourteen	136
One hundred thirty-six	800
Two hundred twenty-two	924
Eight hundred	342

SKILL: Numeral Representation

15. More than One Way

To represent numbers, you can write the **numeral** (284), spell the word (two hundred eighty-four), or write the **expanded form**. To write the expanded form, you add the value of each digit. For example, 200 + 80 + 4 = 284.

➥ COLOR the bubble next to the number that doesn't match.

1. ⭕ 714   ⭕ seven hundred fourteen   ⭕ 70 + 14 + 4

2. ⭕ 863   ⭕ eight hundred thirty-six   ⭕ 800 + 60 + 3

3. ⭕ 400 + 50 + 0   ⭕ four hundred five   ⭕ 450

4. ⭕ three hundred seventy-five ⭕ 300 + 50 + 7 ⭕ 375

5. ⭕ 207   ⭕ two hundred seventy   ⭕ 200 + 70 + 0

➥ WRITE the numeral for each expanded form.

6. 500 + 90 + 1 = _____

7. 700 + 20 + 5 = _____

8. 300 + 40 + 6 = _____

9. 800 + 90 + 1 = _____

10. 400 + 70 + 8 = _____

➥ WRITE the expanded form of each number.

11. _____ + _____ + _____ = 999

12. _____ + _____ + _____ = 565

13. _____ + _____ + _____ = 371

14. _____ + _____ + _____ = 642

15. _____ + _____ + _____ = 183

SKILL: Numeral Representation

16. Alligator Bites

The **greater than** (>), **less than** (<), and **equal** (=) **symbols** are used to compare numbers. To compare a three-digit number, start with the hundreds. If they are equal, compare the tens. If the tens are equal, compare the ones. If all the digits are the same, the two numbers are equal.

To help you to remember which way the symbol goes, imagine a hungry alligator. He always wants the bigger amount!

Compare the amounts. WRITE the correct symbol (>, <, =) in the circle between the two numbers.

795 ◯ 899   245 ◯ 254

863 ◯ 863   377 ◯ 773

552 ◯ 553   408 ◯ 480

458 ◯ 452   702 ◯ 699

603 ◯ 603   400 ◯ 500

999 ◯ 599   300 ◯ 301

197 ◯ 200   507 ◯ 500

309 ◯ 390   169 ◯ 691

212 ◯ 121   888 ◯ 888

303 ◯ 283   990 ◯ 909

SKILL: Comparing Numerals

17. Break It Up

You can break apart numbers into their place value parts to help solve addition problems. Here is an example:

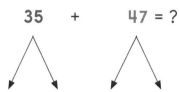

35 + **47** = ?

30 + 5 + 40 + 7
tens ones tens ones

Add the tens: **30** + **40** = 70

Add the ones: **5** + 7 = 12

How many in all? 70 + 12 = 82

Now we know that: 35 + 47 = 82

➡ Break apart the numbers. ADD the numbers back up.

1.   23   +   48 = ?

___ + ___ + ___ + ___
tens ones tens ones

Add the tens: ___ + ___ = ___

Add the ones: ___ + ___ = ___

How many in all? ___ + ___ = ___

Now we know that: 23 + 48 = ___

2.   36   +   36 = ?

___ + ___ + ___ + ___
tens ones tens ones

Add the tens: ___ + ___ = ___

Add the ones: ___ + ___ = ___

How many in all? ___ + ___ = ___

Now we know that: 36 + 36 = ___

3.   48   +   19 = ?

___ + ___ + ___ + ___
tens ones tens ones

Add the tens: ___ + ___ = ___

Add the ones: ___ + ___ = ___

How many in all? ___ + ___ = ___

Now we know that: 48 + 19 = ___

SKILL: Addition and Subtraction

18. Good Neighbors

You can think of two-digit numbers as good neighbors. If you add the ones together and have more than nine, you can share the ten with the other tens next door. When you try to subtract the ones and the first number is smaller than the second, the smaller number can borrow a ten from next door.

➡ SOLVE each problem.

57 + 25	61 − 42	38 + 16	93 − 38
19 + 42	74 − 36	36 + 38	54 − 16
55 + 38	82 − 25	44 + 55	78 − 32
46 + 32	99 − 55	57 + 40	68 − 19

SKILL: Addition and Subtraction

19. Sporty Shopping Spree

You can regroup, break apart, and rearrange numbers to help you add numbers. Here is an example:

Leah is getting ready for soccer. She buys a pair of cleats, a soccer ball, a water bottle, and some socks. How much did she spend?

$55 + 14 + 23 + 36 = $ _____

Break the numbers into tens and ones:
$(50 + 5) + (10 + 4) + (20 + 3) + (30 + 6) = $ _____

Regroup the tens and ones:
$(50 + 10 + 20 + 30) + (5 + 4 + 3 + 6) = $ _____

Now you have: $110 + 18 = $ _____

Break 110 into hundreds and tens and the 18 into tens and ones: $(100 + 10) + (10 + 8) = $ _____

Regroup the tens: $100 + (10 + 10) + 8 = $ _____

Now add the tens and solve! $100 + 20 + 8 = 128$

➡ ADD the items in each box to find the total amount. WRITE the equation and SOLVE using addition strategies on another piece of paper.

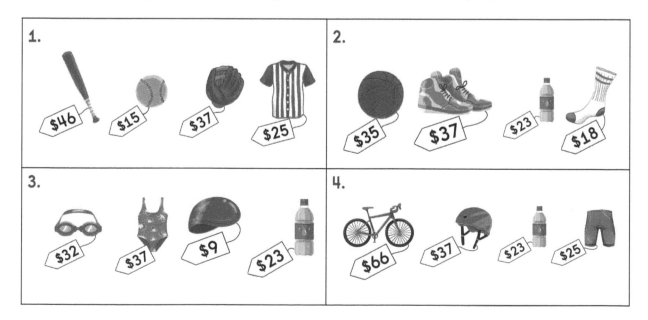

1.
$46 $15 $37 $25

2.
$35 $37 $23 $18

3.
$32 $37 $9 $23

4.
$66 $37 $23 $25

20. It All Adds Up!

There is more than one way to represent numbers. Numbers can be regrouped, broken apart, and rearranged. When you put the pieces back together, the number is the same!

➡ DRAW a line to connect equal amounts.

23 + 38 + 14 + 18

36 12 29 + 4

29 + 42 + 16 + 31

(10 + 60 + 30 + 10) + (7 + 5 + 6)

116

(40 + 5) + (10 + 6) + (20 + 8) + (30 + 6)

(30 + 10 + 20) + (6 + 2 + 9 + 4)

128

45 + 16 + 28 + 36

29 42 16 + 31

(20 + 3) + (30 + 8) + (10 + 4) + (10 + 8)

(40 + 20 + 10 + 30) + (5 + 9 + 2)

SKILL: Addition

21. Math Super Star

Once you know how to add and subtract 2-digit numbers, adding larger numbers will be easy! You are a Math Super Star!

➡ SOLVE the equations. WRITE your answer in the space provided.

```
   347          861          403          945
  +285         -742         +279         -742
```

```
   506          279          299          683
  +391         -122         +105         -245
```

```
   604          718          643          912
  +366         -143         +208         -152
```

SKILL: Addition and Subtraction

22. Which Tool to Choose?

Length is the measurement of how long something is from one end to the other. Rulers, yardsticks, meter sticks, and measuring tapes are tools used to measure things. A **ruler** is 12 inches (or 1 foot) long. A **yard stick** is 36 inches (or 3 feet) long. A **meter stick** is 100 centimeters long. A **measuring tape** can show length in inches or centimeters. Some measuring tapes are flexible so you can measure around something.

➡ DRAW a line to connect the measuring tool you would use to measure each object. You can use a tool more than once.

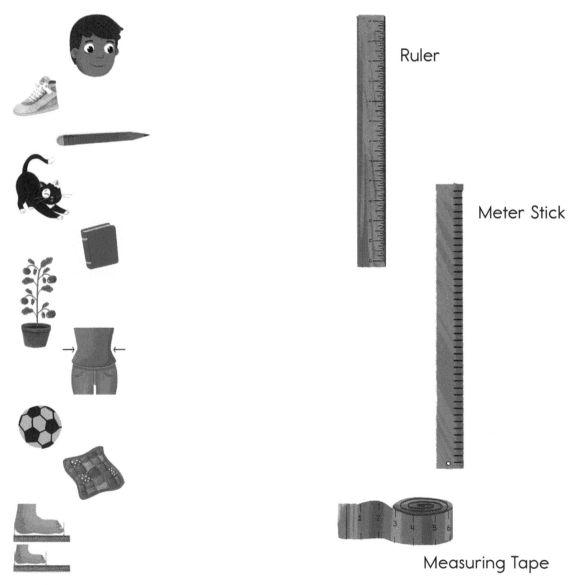

Ruler

Meter Stick

Measuring Tape

23. How Much Longer?

Standard units of measure are always the same length. **Centimeters, inches, feet, meters,** and **yards** are examples of standard units of measure. When you compare the length of two or more objects, you need to use the same unit of measure.

➡ MEASURE the objects using inches or centimeters. WRITE and solve an equation to show the difference between the two lengths in **standard units of measure.**

1.

How long is the pencil? _____ centimeters

How long is the crayon? _____ centimeters

How much longer is the pencil? _____

2.

How long is the paper clip? _____ inches

How long is the marker? _____ inches

How much longer is the marker? _____

3.

How long is the eraser? _____ inches

How long is the chalk? _____ inches

What is the difference in length between the two objects?

_____

SKILL: Measuring Length

24. At the Fair

It is important to use the same **standard unit of measure** when comparing measurements.

➡ READ each question. COLOR the bubble next to the answer.

1. Janelle is 42 inches tall. To ride on the roller coaster, you need to be 48 inches tall. How much taller does Janelle need to be to go on the ride?
   ○ 3 inches   ○ 6 inches   ○ 12 inches

2. A large box of popcorn is 12 inches high and a small box is 8 inches high. How much bigger is the large box of popcorn?
   ○ 4 inches   ○ 20 inches   ○ 6 inches

3. The line to go on the Ferris wheel is 51 feet long. The line to go on the merry-go-round is 36 feet long. What is the difference between the two lines?
   ○ 12 inches   ○ 87 feet   ○ 15 feet

4. The tall man is 8 feet tall. The acrobat is 5 feet tall. How much taller is the tall man?
   ○ 3 yards   ○ 3 feet   ○ 3 inches

5. The fluffy chicks in the farm tent are 12 centimeters tall. The chickens are 45 centimeters tall. How much taller are the chickens?
   ○ 33 inches   ○ 3 feet   ○ 33 centimeters

6. Manuel's prize is 2 feet long. Li won a prize that is 4 feet long. How much longer is Li's prize?
   ○ 2 inches   ○ 2 feet   ○ 6 meters

7. The big slide is 84 feet long. The little slide is 27 feet long. What is the difference between the two slides?
   ○ 57 feet   ○ 111 feet   ○ 47 meters

8. The deluxe two-day pass is 21 centimeters long. The one-day pass is 13 centimeters long. How much longer is the deluxe pass?
   ○ 8 inches   ○ 34 centimeters ○ 8 centimeters

SKILL: Measuring Length

25. Ready, Set, Measure!

A **unit of measure** is what you use to measure something with. You can use a paper clip, your shoe, or even your hand to measure something. If you measured a desk with your hand, it might be 12 hands long. If a grown-up measured the same desk, it might be only 8 hands long. How can a desk be two different measurements? It is because your hand is probably smaller than a grown-up's hand, so it would take more of your hands to measure the same object. **Standard units of measure** are *always* the same length. **Centimeters, inches, feet, meters,** and **yards** are examples of standard units of measure.

➡ Use the ruler and paper clip below to measure about how long the following things around your home are.

1. A book is _____ inches or _____ paper clips long.

2. A hand towel is _____ inches or _____ paper clips long.

3. A phone is _____ centimeters or _____ paper clips long

4. My sneaker is _____ inches or _____ paper clips long.

5. A toothbrush is _____ centimeters or _____ paper clips long.

6. My pillow is _____ inches or _____ paper clips long.

7. A pencil is _____ centimeters or _____ paper clips long.

8. A box of cereal is _____ centimeters or _____ paper clips long.

9. An envelope is _____ inches or _____ paper clips long.

10. A key is _____ centimeters or _____ paper clips long.

11. Was the length in paper clips **>**, **<**, or **=** to the length in inches? _____

12. Was the length in paper clips **>**, **<**, or **=** to the length in centimeters? _____

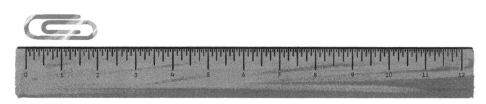

SKILL: Measuring Length

26. How to Measure a Whale

Centimeters and inches are used to measure small things like books, plants, or hamsters. Feet, yards, and meters are used to measure bigger things like beds, swimming pools, or houses. When you measure something, choose the **standard unit of measure** that makes sense. It wouldn't make sense to measure a whale in centimeters!

➡ CIRCLE the best unit of measure to find out the length of each object.

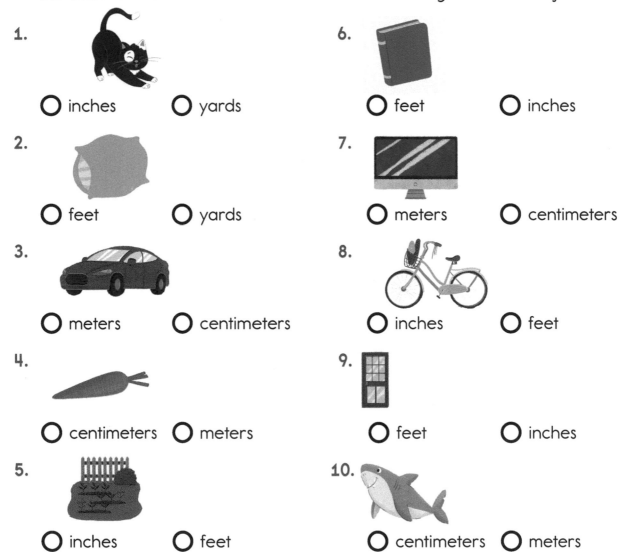

1.

○ inches   ○ yards

2.

○ feet   ○ yards

3.

○ meters   ○ centimeters

4.

○ centimeters ○ meters

5.

○ inches   ○ feet

6.

○ feet   ○ inches

7.

○ meters   ○ centimeters

8.

○ inches   ○ feet

9.

○ feet   ○ inches

10.

○ centimeters ○ meters

SKILL: Units of Measurement

27. Best Guess

An **estimate** is a best guess. It doesn't have to be exact. To estimate a length, guess an amount that is about, close to, near, or almost the actual length. To measure an elephant, you would probably use feet or yards and not inches!
➠ LOOK at each picture. DRAW a line to your best estimate of how long it is.

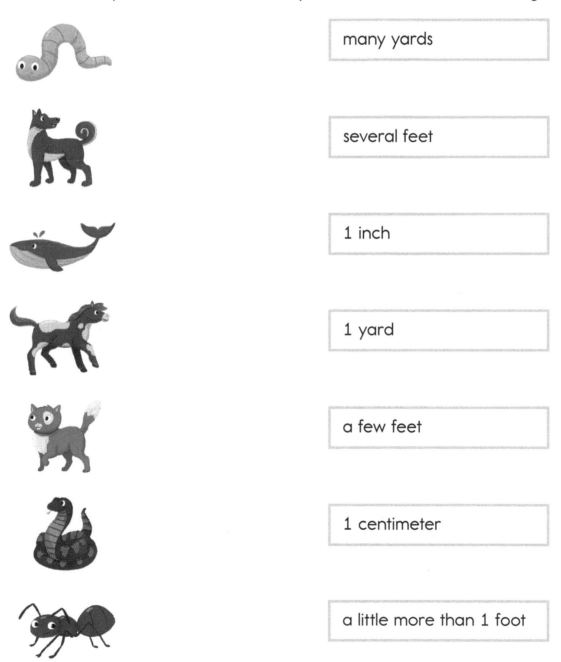

many yards

several feet

1 inch

1 yard

a few feet

1 centimeter

a little more than 1 foot

28. Spring Planting

You sometimes need to add and subtract lengths to solve real-life problems.
➡ LOOK at the picture to help solve the problems. WRITE an equation for each question and SOLVE.

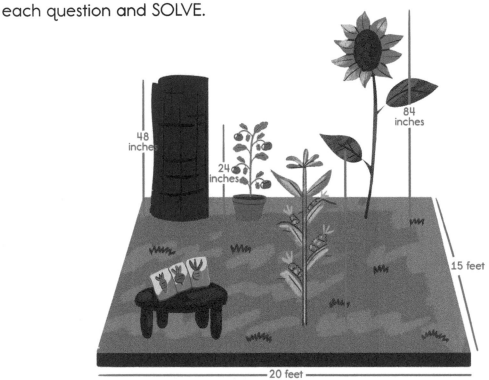

1. Farmer Eton is planting a garden. His garden is 20 feet by 15 feet. How much fencing will he need to go around the whole garden? _____

2. How much taller are the sunflowers than the fence? _____

3. Farmer Eton needs to cut poles for the beans. Each pole needs to be 29 inches long. How long of a pole will he need to buy to cut three bean poles? _____

4. How much shorter is the tomato plant than the corn plant? _____

5. Farmer Eton plants 18 feet of carrot seeds, 15 feet of beet seeds, and 19 feet of radish seeds. How many feet of seeds did he plant altogether? _____

6. If the tomato plant grows 9 more inches, how tall will it be?

SKILL: Adding and Subtracting Lengths

29. Measuring the Animal Kingdom

When adding and subtracting lengths, the units of measurement must be the same.

➡ WRITE the equation and then SOLVE.

1. A gorilla was 36 inches tall on her first birthday. She was 53 inches tall on her next birthday. How many inches did she grow in a year?

2. A humpback whale is 49 feet long. A killer whale is 25 feet long. How much longer is the humpback whale?

3. A mother giraffe is 19 feet tall. Her baby is 7 feet tall. How much taller is the mother giraffe?

4. A kangaroo jumped 23 feet in one hop, 21 feet in the second hop, and 24 feet in the third hop. How far did the kangaroo jump?

5. The cheetah ran 81 meters before finding food. For his next meal, he ran 78 meters. How many fewer meters did he run for his second meal?

6. An adult elephant's tusk is 72 inches long. A baby's tusk is 24 inches long. How much longer is an adult elephant's tusk?

7. A worm crawled 26 inches on Monday, 36 inches on Tuesday, and 22 inches on Wednesday. How many inches did it crawl altogether?

SKILL: Adding and Subtracting Lengths

30. Playground Fun

Rulers, yardsticks, and measuring tapes are like number lines. If you need to add or subtract lengths, using a **number line** can help you to figure out a problem. Here is an example:

Mia jumped 5 feet and Jenna jumped 3 feet. How much farther did Mia jump?

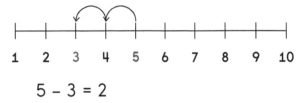

1 2 3 4 5 6 7 8 9 10

5 – 3 = 2

➡ SOLVE the problems using the number line. SHOW your work on the number lines. WRITE the equation.

1. Jorge climbed the tall jungle gym. He climbed 11 feet from the ground to the middle tower. He then climbed 6 feet from the middle tower to the tall tower. How many feet did he climb in all? _____

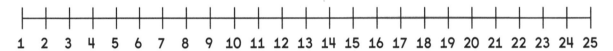

1 2 3 4 5 6 7 8 9 10 11 12 13 14 15 16 17 18 19 20 21 22 23 24 25

2. The first set of monkey bars is 8 feet long. The next set is 13 feet long. How long are the monkey bars altogether? _____

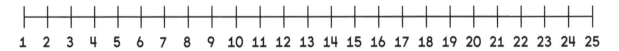

1 2 3 4 5 6 7 8 9 10 11 12 13 14 15 16 17 18 19 20 21 22 23 24 25

3. The toddler slide is 3 feet off the ground. The big-kid slide is 8 feet tall. What is the difference between the two slides? _____

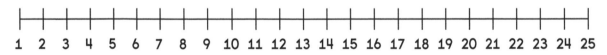

1 2 3 4 5 6 7 8 9 10 11 12 13 14 15 16 17 18 19 20 21 22 23 24 25

4. Karin rolled 15 yards down a hill. Lee rolled 3 yards farther than Karin. How far did Lee roll? _____

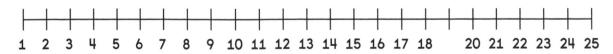

1 2 3 4 5 6 7 8 9 10 11 12 13 14 15 16 17 18   20 21 22 23 24 25

SKILL: Number Line

31. Carpenter Caper

You can make your own **number line** to help solve problems. For addition, put the larger number at the *beginning* of the number line and count up from there. For subtraction, put the larger number at the *end* of the number line and count backwards from there.

➡ READ each problem. WRITE the numbers on the number line. WRITE and solve the equations.

1. A carpenter is installing a door. It is 54 inches wide and 84 inches tall. What is the difference between the height and the width?

_____

2. The distance between the door and the light switch is 49 inches. The distance between the light switch and the window is 28 inches. How far is the window from the door?

_____

3. It is 10 feet from the first floor to the second floor. It is 9 feet from the second floor to the attic floor. How many feet is it from the first floor to the attic?

_____

4. The garage door is 21 feet wide. The front door is 5 feet wide. What is the difference between the two widths?

_____

32. Tick Tock, Tick Tock

Clocks are tools used to measure time.

An **analog clock** has two "hands" that look like arrows. The little hand points to the hours and the big hand points to the minutes.

A **digital clock** displays the hours and minutes like this: Hours : Minutes.

Both of these clocks show 8:25.

➡ DRAW a line to connect matching times on the analog and digital clocks.

03:30   02:00   03:45   10:35   04:45

07:20   01:40   08:10   07:55   06:05

SKILL: Time

33. Lucy's Busy Day

An **analog clock** tells the time and shows the passage of time as the hands move around the clock. A day is 24 hours long. The smaller hour hand goes around the clock two times each day. If something happened between midnight and noon, we write **a.m.** after the time. If it happened between noon and midnight, we write **p.m.** after the time.

➡ WRITE the time or DRAW the hands on the clock to show the time each event happened. Remember to write the time to show a.m. or p.m.!

1. Lucy woke up at 7:45 a.m.

2. What time did Lucy have breakfast?

_____

3. Lucy had a picnic lunch with Bear at 12:15 p.m.

4. What time did Lucy play soccer? _____

5. Lucy took a bath after dinner at 7:00 p.m.

6. What time did Lucy fall asleep? _____

SKILL: Time

34. Piggy Bank Savings

When we buy something, we pay for it in amounts of dollars and cents. The symbol for dollars is **$** and the symbol for cents is **¢**.

1 dollar $1.00
$1.00 = 100¢

1 quarter   25¢
4 quarters = $1.00

1 dime   10¢
10 dimes = $1.00

1 nickel 5¢
20 nickels = $1.00

1 penny   1¢
100 cents = $1.00

➡ ADD the bills and coins. DRAW a line to connect the amount to the matching piggy bank.

1 dollar bill, 3 quarters, 1 dime, two nickels, and 1 penny	$ 2.44
1 dollar, 4 quarters, 3 dimes, 1 nickel, and 9 pennies	$ 2.10
1 dollar, 1 quarter, 10 dimes, 4 nickels, and 1 penny	$ 2.50
1 dollar, 2 quarters, 3 dimes, 4 nickels, and 10 pennies	$ 1.96
1 dollar, 3 quarters, 4 dimes, 6 nickels, and 5 pennies	$ 2.46

SKILL: Money

35. Beach Shop

To show dollars and cents in numbered amounts, we write dollars to the left of the **.** and cents to the right. The dollar sign (**$**) is used for amounts greater than 99 cents. The cents sign (**¢**) is used for amounts less than one dollar.

Eighty-nine cents = 89¢   One dollar and fifty-six cents = $1.56

➡ ADD the bills and coins. WRITE the **amount** and the correct **symbol**. CIRCLE your answer to the question.

1.

How much money do you have? _____

Do you have enough money to buy the beach ball? YES   NO

2.

How much money do you have? _____

Do you have enough money to buy the sunglasses? YES   NO

3.

How much money do you have? _____

Do you have enough money to buy the sunscreen lotion?
YES   NO

4.

How much money do you have? _____

Do you have enough money to buy the pail and shovel?
YES   NO

SKILL: Money

36. How Does Your Garden Grow?

A **graph** gives you information about the whole group. A **line plot** is one kind of graph.

Example:

The 20 children in Ms. Abram's Garden Club planted bean seeds. This line plot shows the height of each child's plant. Each x represents the height of one child's plant.

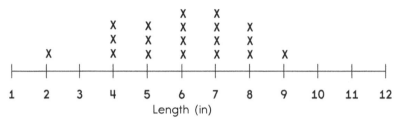

➡ HELP the garden club graph their plants on the line plots below.

Tomato Plants

One month after planting them, 6 tomato plants are 9 inches tall, 4 tomato plants are 6 inches tall, 2 tomato plants are 7 inches tall, 3 tomato plants are 8 inches tall, and 5 tomato plants are 5 inches tall.

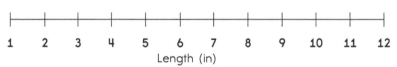

Pepper Plants

After two weeks, 4 plants are 1 centimeter tall, 5 plants are 2 centimeters tall, 7 plants are 5 centimeters tall, 1 plant is 3 centimeters tall, and 3 plants are 4 centimeters tall.

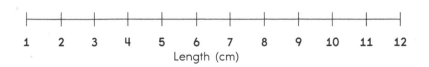

SKILL: Data Representation

37. Getting Good at Graphing

A **picture graph** uses pictures or symbols to compare data. A **bar graph** compares data using bars.

Picture Graph
Favorite Sports to Play

Bar Graph
Favorite Sports to Watch

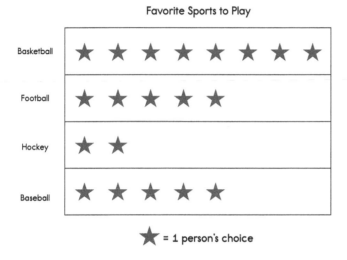

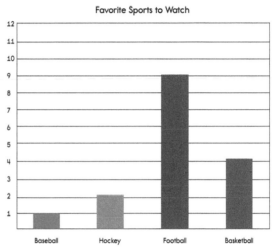

★ = 1 person's choice

➡ LOOK at each graph. ANSWER the questions.

1. What sport is the most popular to play? _____

2. What sport is the most popular to watch? _____

3. How many people like to watch football most? _____

4. How many people like to play football most? _____

5. How many more people like to watch football than hockey? _____

6. How many fewer people like to play hockey than baseball? _____

7. Do more people like to play hockey or watch hockey? _____

8. How many more people like to watch football than play football? _____

9. How many people were surveyed? _____

38. Getting in Shape

Shapes have **attributes** that make them different from other shapes. **Edges**, or **sides**, and **angles**, or **corners**, are shape attributes. Edges are connected to angles.
➡ WRITE the number of **edges** and **angles** for each shape below. WRITE an example of where you might see the shape in real life.

Shape	Name	Number of Edges	Number of Angles	Real-Life Example
○	circle			
△	triangle			
□	square			
▭	rectangle			
⏢	trapezoid			
⬠	pentagon			

SKILL: Shape Attributes

39. Quadrilateral Quiz

Categories of shapes share attributes. A **quadrilateral** is a four-sided shape. There are many different kinds of quadrilaterals. Here are some you may be familiar with:

> **square, rectangle, parallelogram, rhombus, trapezoid, kite**

➡ If the shape is a **quadrilateral**, COLOR it **red**. If it is not, color it **blue**. Three in a row is tic-tac-toe!

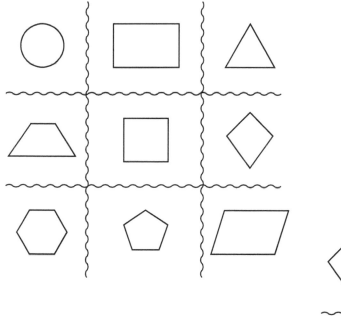

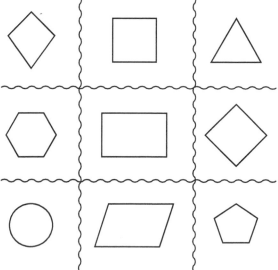

40. The Shape of Things

Circles, triangles, quadrilaterals, pentagons, and hexagons are **two-dimensional shapes**. They are flat and have two dimensions: width and length. **Three-dimensional shapes** have length, width, and height. They can have flat and/or curved surfaces. Here are some examples:

A **sphere** is a circular shape that is round like a ball.

A **cone** is a triangular shape that looks like an ice cream cone.

A **cube** looks like a box.

➡ READ the words in the box. WRITE the name of the shape under each picture. (Two of the words will be used twice).

> circle, triangle, square, rectangle, pentagon,
> hexagon, cone, sphere, cube, diamond

_____

_____

_____

_____

_____

_____

_____

_____

_____

_____

_____

_____

SKILL: Shape Attributes

41. Quilting Bee

You can **partition**, which means to divide or separate, a rectangle into rows and columns to make equal shares. Rows are **horizontal**, meaning they go from side to side. **Columns** are vertical, meaning they go up and down. Each row and column needs to be spaced evenly.

➡ FOLLOW the instructions below.

1. Color the quilt that is partitioned into 5 rows and 4 columns.

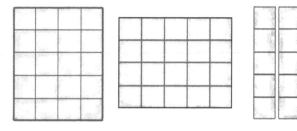

2. Color the quilt that is partitioned into 3 rows and 5 columns.

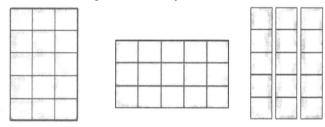

3. How many rows in the quilt on the right? _____

   How many columns? _____

   How many square patches does the quilt have? _____

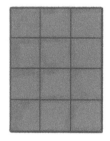

4. Partition the rectangle into 4 rows and 6 columns.
   How many patches does this quilt have? _____

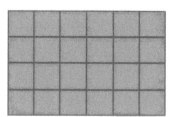

42. Community Garden

A rectangle can be partitioned into equal shares by dividing it into evenly spaced rows and columns. Rows run horizontally from side to side. Columns run vertically up and down.

➡ PARTITION the gardens into equal shares, then COUNT the squares.

1.

4 rows and 4 columns

How many equal shares? _____

2.

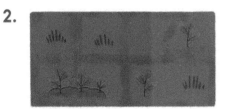

2 rows and 4 columns

How many equal shares? _____

3.

5 rows and 3 columns

How many equal shares? _____

4.

1 rows and 6 columns

How many equal shares? _____

5.

3 rows and 2 columns

How many equal shares? _____

6.

3 rows and 3 columns

How many equal shares? _____

SKILL: Equal Shares

43. Fair Share

Shapes can be divided into equal shares. If a shape has two equal parts, the parts are described as **halves**. If a shape has three equal parts, the parts are described as **thirds**. If a shape has four equal parts, the parts are described as **fourths** or **quarters**.

➡ DRAW a line to divide the shapes into equal shares.

4 equal parts

Fourths

Halves

Halves

2 equal parts

Thirds

6 equal parts

3 equal parts

Halves

SKILL: Equal Shares

44. Even Steven

Equal shares of matching wholes do not need to have the same shape. For example, a square can be divided into four equal shares by drawing a cross in the middle, by drawing an X in the middle, or by drawing four equal rows.

➡ DRAW lines to partition the rectangles into equal shares in two different ways.

1. Halves

2. Fourths

3. Fourths

4. Thirds

5. Thirds

SKILL: Equal Shares

45. Dividing Line

If a shape has two equal parts, the parts are called **halves**. If a shape has three equal parts, the parts are called **thirds**. If a shape has four equal parts, the parts are called **fourths**.

➥ LOOK at each colored shape. READ the directions below each shape. COLOR the parts.

1. Color two halves.

2. Color two thirds.

3. Color three fourths.

4. Color one third.

5. Color two thirds.

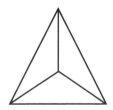

6. Color two thirds.

7. Color one half.

8. Color one fourth.

9. Color one fourth.

10. Color one third.

SKILL: Equal Shares

Answer Key

Part 1: Reading

1. Valuable Vowels

Short Vowel Words: jump, pin, dress, bat, fox, pet, bell, cap, bug, bus, hand, frog, ring

Long Vowel Words: snow, snake, blue, bike, night, bee, home, see, boat, kite, June, rain

2. Listen Carefully

Puzzle 1:

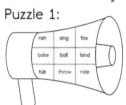

Puzzle 2:

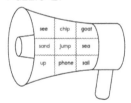

3. Ship Ahoy!

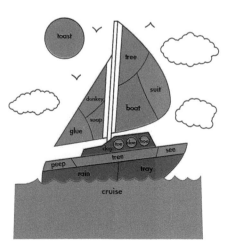

4. Team Spirit

I hear a long vowel sound: pail, day, tea, three, key, pie, goat, toe, true, suit, feud

I hear a special sound: sauce, eight, soon, voice, toy, loud, buy

5. Teamwork

1. au: laundry   2. oo: moon
3. oy: boy   4. oi: coin   5. ou cloud
6. au: faucet   7. ou: house   8. oi: boil

6. Dream Team

1. pain   2. blue   3. pool   4. join
5. day   6. bee   7. cloud   8. freight
9. meat   10. money   11. float
12. boy   13. fruit   14. sail
15. dream

7. Clap to the Beat

1. for | est   2. rain | bow   3. gar | den
4. el | bow   5. tur | tle   6. drag | on
7. cup | cake   8. doc | tor
9. can | dle   10. bas | ket
11. snow | man   12. mar | ble

8. Harvest Time

Summer is over and fall is here. It is **harvest** time! Ripe red **apples** are ready for picking. The **garden** is bursting with vegetables. Hop, hop, hop! A **bunny** tries to steal a bright orange **carrot**. "Go away!" cries the **farmer**. A **scarecrow** watches over the fields. Corn, **pumpkins**, and squash need to be picked, too. At the end of a busy day, the farmer will play her **fiddle** as the sun sets over the farm.

9. Dividing Line

1. pi | lot   2. drag | on
3. cab | in   4. fro | zen
5. sal | ad   6. pi | rate   7. mu | sic
8. a | pron   9. pa | per
10. ho | tel

10. Tiger vs. Camel

Tiger (v | cv): be | gin; ba | ker;
o | pen; spi | der; a | corn; mu | sic;
pa | per; e | ven; Fri | day; fla | vor

Camel (vc | v): nev | er; lem | on;
vis | it; sev | en; dam | age; hab | it;
plan | et; mon | ey; tal | ent; pal | ace

11. Prefix Preview

1. unhappy   2. incomplete
3. misbehave   4. reappear
5. unclean   6. disobey   7. misspell
8. preheat   9. dishonest   10. redo

12. Unafraid!

13. Super Suffixes

1. ed   2. less   3. ly   4. s   5. er
6. est   7. ful   8. es   9. y   10. ing

14. Beginnings and Endings

Puzzle 1:

Puzzle 2:

15. Do You Hear a Bear?

bear, snow, touch, moon, soup, tear, tie,
book, piece, cow, hear, loud

16. Mother Robin's Nest

Answers may vary.

1. The story is about Mother Robin.
2. Mother Robin is building a nest.
3. The nest will be built in a tree.
4. The nest will be built in
   the spring.
5. Mother Robin needs a place to
   lay her eggs.
6. The nest will be made by
   collecting soft grass and twigs
   and pressing them into a
   cup shape.

17. A Dog for Geo

1. Geo   2. a dog   3. They think
Geo is too young to care for a
dog.   4. Geo takes care of other
dogs.   5. the animal shelter   6. on
his tenth birthday

18. The Lion and the Mouse

You are never too small to be a big help.

19. Telling Tales

Paragraph 1: Folktales are stories that are retold many times.

Paragraph 2: Fables are short folktales that teach a life lesson or moral.

Paragraph 3: Fairy tales are magical stories about good vs. evil.

20. Sharp Focus

Top Line: Answers will vary.

Paragraph 1: The Statue of Liberty Stands for Freedom

Paragraph 2: Building the Statue of Liberty

Paragraph 3: Visiting the Statue of Liberty

21. Very Inventive

1. inventions
2. introducing inventions
3. inventions build on each other
4. accidental inventions

22. Focus Finder

1. 3
2. All
3. 2
4. 1

23. Saving the Everglades

Many people believed that the Everglades was a useless swamp. → The land was drained . . .

Marjory Stoneman Douglas gave speeches . . . → Everglades National Park was created.

Cities and houses were built on Everglades land. → The animals were losing their homes.

24. Basketball Now and Then

Answers will vary.

25. A Treat for the Birds

To make a pine cone bird feeder, **first** tie the string around the top of the pine cone. **Next**, spread the peanut butter all over the surface of the pine cone using the craft stick. **After that**, pour the birdseed into the bowl and roll the pine cone over the birdseed. **Last**, hang your feeder on a branch near a window so that you can watch the birds come to the feeder. 3 1 2 4

26. Gold Rush

The gold seekers needed supplies. → Merchants opened businesses that sold . . .

Miners often ripped their pants. → Mr. Davis invented sturdy pants.

Mr. Davis didn't have enough money. → Mr. Davis teamed up with Mr. Strauss . . .

27. Best Camping Trip Ever

<u>4</u> Dad had an idea. He suggested camping inside.

<u>2</u> Just before they packed the car, the sky turned dark and gray. A crack of thunder shook the house. It was followed by a streak of lightning and pouring rain.

<u>6</u> "This is the best camping trip ever!" said Shen. Everyone agreed. "Can we do it again next weekend?" asked Lee just before she fell asleep.

<u>1</u> All week long, Shen and Lee were looking forward to going camping with their parents. Their bags were packed, and they were ready to go.

<u>5</u> They set up their tent in the living room and roasted marshmallows in the fireplace. Mom played her guitar, and everyone sang along.

<u>3</u> Everyone was disappointed. Now they couldn't go camping.

28. A Day With Balloons

1. → 4
2. → 1
3. → 5
4. → 2
5. → 3

29. Alliteration Alphabet
Answers will vary.

30. Dear Diary

1. Marina
2. both
3. Tina
4. Marina
5. both

31. City Mouse, Country Mouse
Answers will vary, but generally should show that City Mouse likes fancy things and Country Mouse prefers simple things.

32. Life in the Forest

1. → g
2. → f
3. → h
4. → e
5. → d
6. → b
7. → a
8. → c

33. Look for the Clues!

1. rain
2. sizzling
3. dry
4. changed
5. hold or keep
6. water
7. animals killed to eat
8. chance

34. Solar System Study

1. astronaut
2. planet
3. telescope
4. moon
5. universe
6. gravity

35. Special Features

1. caption
2. glossary
3. graph
4. table of contents

36. Recycled Reasons

Recycling → inform

Mayville Recycles → persuade

Ruth Recycles → entertain

37. Reading the Clues
1. winter
2. loudly
3. white
4. swim
5. mountains
6. night

38. Sly Sam
1. a cat
2. sneaky
3. Sam
4. under the couch cushion

39. Blow, Wind, Blow
1. wind turbine
2. generator
3. wind farms
4. blades
5. electricity
6. fans

40. What Kind of Pie?
1. apple
2. 24
3. chocolate cream
4. Answers will vary; something about how the class will have a difficult time deciding what kind of pizza to make.
5. Answers will vary but should express that Mr. Kim could survey the class to find out what kind of pizza they like best and then represent the data with a pizza pie chart.

41. Kindness Matters
Answers will vary.

42. Festival of Colors
Written answers will vary.

1. both 2. both 3. both
4. All About Holi 5. both

43. Pets for Children
1. yes
2. yes
3. no
4. yes
5. yes

44. Kangaroos
1. both
2. Baby Joey
3. All About Kangaroos
4. both
5. All About Kangaroos
6. All About Kangaroos

45. Slow and Steady
1. different
2. different
3. same
4. same
5. same

Part 2: Writing

1. A Litter of Puppies
1. dozen 2. pack 3. bunch
4. team 5. band 6. bouquet
7. class 8. flock 9. batch 10. stack
11. collection 12. pair

2. A Gaggle of Geese
1. a <u>pod</u> of whales
2. a <u>pride</u> of lions
3. a <u>pack</u> of wolves

4. a <u>colony</u> of bats
5. a <u>caravan</u> of camels
6. a <u>litter</u> of kittens
7. a <u>swarm</u> of bees
8. a <u>mob</u> of kangaroos
9. a <u>flock</u> of sheep
10. a <u>nest</u> of mice
11. a <u>school</u> of dolphins
12. a <u>crash</u> of rhinoceroses
13. a <u>scurry</u> of squirrels
14. a <u>family</u> of beavers
15. a <u>sloth</u> of bears
16. a <u>band</u> of gorillas
17. a <u>prickle</u> of porcupines
18. a <u>wisdom</u> of wombats
19. a <u>zeal</u> of zebras
20. a <u>lounge</u> of lizards

3. Making More

1. sandwiches   2. flowers   3. women
4. geese   5. cows   6. birds
7. tomatoes   8. wolves   9. dishes
10. moose   11. monsters   12. boxes

4. Rule Breakers

foot → feet; fish → fish; child → children; mouse → mice; man → men; leaf → leaves; scarf → scarves; tooth → teeth; ox → oxen; deer → deer; person → people; moose → moose

5. Test Your Reflexes

1. <u>Peter</u>; (himself)   2. <u>children</u>; (themselves)   3. <u>We</u>; (ourselves)
4. <u>I</u>; (myself)   5. <u>You</u>; (yourself)
6. <u>Julie and I</u>; (ourselves)   7. <u>The bird</u>; (itself)   8. <u>She</u>; (herself)
9. <u>I</u>; (myself)   10. <u>My sister</u>; (herself)
11. <u>They</u>; (themselves)
12. <u>The dragon</u>; (itself)

6. Reflexology

1. herself   2. myself   3. ourselves
4. themselves   5. himself   6. itself
7. yourself
BONUS: Answers will vary.

7. Now and Then

Puzzle 1:

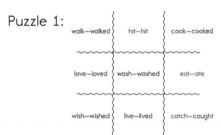

Puzzle 2:

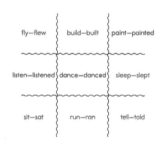

8. Past and Present

write → wrote; go → went; sit → sat; run → ran; eat → ate; teach → taught; fly → flew; hit → hit; bring → brought; sleep → slept; begin → began; find → found; write → wrote; come → came; feel → felt; break → broke; have → had; give → gave; meet → met; say → said

9. Describing Words

kitten; soft

pig; muddy

chickens; many

rainbow; beautiful

cow; spotted

sells; weekly

crows; noisily

runs; quickly

milks; carefully

win; likely

10. Adjective or Adverb?

1. adverb
2. adjective
3. adjective
4. adverb
5. adverb
6. adjective
7. adverb
8. adjective
9. adjective
10. adverb
11. adverb
12. adverb

11. Paint a Picture!
Answers will vary.

12. Build a Better Sentence
Answers will vary.

13. Scrambled Eggs for Breakfast

1. Statement: <u>Jose will make scrambled eggs for breakfast.</u>
   Question: <u>Will Jose make scrambled eggs for breakfast?</u>

2. Statement: <u>Dad can make some coffee.</u>
   Question: <u>Can Dad make some coffee?</u>

3. Statement: <u>Mom will make some crispy bacon.</u>
   Question: <u>Will Mom make some crispy bacon?</u>

4. Statement: <u>Mia would like jam on her toast.</u>
   Question: <u>Would Mia like jam on her toast?</u>

5. Statement: <u>Cory should pour the orange juice.</u>
   Question: <u>Should Cory pour the orange juice?</u>

14. Joining Together

1. O Airi walks her dog and cat.
   O Airi walks her dog.
   O Airi feeds her cat.
   O Airi takes care of her dog and cat.

2. **O Edward likes to play golf.**
   O Edward likes to play tennis.
   O He does not like to play tennis.
   O Edward likes to play golf and tennis.

3. O It is fun to ride a bike!
   O Riding a bike is difficult but fun.
   O It is so much fun once you learn!
   O Learning to ride a bike is difficult.

4. O I will play basketball.
   O I will practice shooting baskets.
   O I can help my team win the game.
   O Shooting baskets takes practice.

5. O My dog is hungry.
   O I am going to feed my dog.
   O I have to feed my dog.
   O He will be hungry.

15. Very Proper

Puzzle 1:

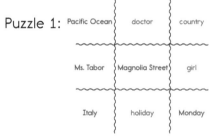

Puzzle 2:

16. Visiting the Capital

The Morez family is going on a trip to Washington, DC. Their plane is leaving on the first Saturday in April. They are going to the National Cherry Blossom Festival. The beautiful pink trees were a gift from Japan. They will see a parade, hear the Jazzy Trio play at the Kennedy Center, and visit the Washington Monument. On Monday, they will take a Super Speedy Scooter tour of the city. On Tuesday, they will visit the Lincoln Memorial, where Martin Luther King Jr. gave his famous speech. On Wednesday, they will have lunch at the Capital Burger Restaurant with Aunt Maria. She will take them to see the National Air and Space Museum in the afternoon. On Thursday, they will visit the Smithsonian National Museum of American History. On Friday, they will have to fly home to Boston. Before they go to the airport, they will take a family picture in front of the United States Capitol building to remember the fun time they had on their vacation.

17. Lists and Letters

1. March 10, 2008
2. My dog likes to play with balls, Frisbees, and sticks.
3. correct
4. correct
5. Sincerely, Georgia
6. correct
7. Simone is good at lacrosse, basketball, and soccer.
8. Dear Ms. Quigley,

18. Three Wishes

Answers will vary. Check comma usage.

19. On Vacation

1. I've
2. they're
3. don't
4. hasn't
5. we'd
6. I'm
7. let's
8. she'd
9. couldn't
10. you're
11. they'll

20. Whose Shoes?

the shoes of my friend →
my friend's shoes

the garden of Mr. Batistini →
Mr. Batistini's garden

the toys of the twins → **the twins' toys**

the apples of the tree →
the tree's apples

the food of the kitten →
the kitten's food

the hive of the bees → **the bees' hive**

the cave of the dragon →
the dragon's cave

the football team of the boy →
the boy's football team

the car of Dr. McMahon →
Dr. McMahon's car

the playground of the children →
the children's playground

the father of Miguel → **Miguel's father**

the game of Jake → **Jake's game**

the book of Winny → **Winny's book**

the tools of the carpenters →
the carpenters' tools

the parents of the girls →
the girls' parents

21. Turtle Dance

22. Keeping Quiet

1. **r**h**ino**
2. ba**dg**e
3. s**c**issors
4. **w**reath
5. tw**o**
6. i**s**land
7. **w**h**a**le
8. cas**t**le
9. lam**b**
10. **k**not
11. **w**h**i**stle
12. **ch**al**k**

23. *R* Is for *Ruler*

1. ran
2. tear
3. rip
4. road
5. trim
6. made
7. read
8. his
9. rush
10. cut

24. Double Trouble

run	√	√	√	ing	running
help	√	√	X	er	helper
jump	√	√	X	ing	jumping
trip	√	√	√	ed	tripped
shop	√	√	√	ing	shopping
thin	√	√	√	est	thinnest
swim	√	√	√	er	swimmer
build	√	X	X	ing	building
sleep	√	X	√	ing	sleeping
clap	√	√	√	ed	clapped
fast	√	√	X	est	fastest
hug	√	√	√	ing	hugging

25. Truck Stop

Puzzle 1:

Puzzle 2:

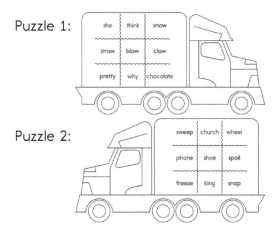

26. What Do You Hear Here?

1. scents
2. sell
3. bear
4. flour
5. Our
6. right
7. sale

8. tail
9. wait
10. too
11. won
12. knight; night

27. Teaming Up

Long Vowel Sound: float, feet, play, beach, train, say, boat, pie, toe, blue, pain, teach, dream

Special Sound: house, coin, cloud, moon, boil, pool, mouse

28. Hey, How's it Going?

1. informal   2. formal   3. informal
4. formal   5. informal   6. formal
7. formal   8. informal

Part 2: (Answers may vary slightly.)

1. What are we going to do after dinner?
2. Thank you for the present.
3. How are you all doing today?
4. I have got to go home now.

29. Baseball Barbecue

1. yearly
2. place where people live
3. helpers
4. give for free
5. pay for
6. guesses that something might happen
7. lucky
8. accomplishment

30. A Piece of Cake

1. g
2. a
3. f
4. c
5. j
6. d

7. e
8. h
9. b
10. i

31. Know It All

1. un; not locked
2. mis; not trust
3. re; visit again
4. dis; not agree
5. in; not correct
6. pre; before school
7. re; fill again
8. mis; not understand
9. un; not fair
10. re; do again

32. Prefix Practice

Puzzle 1:

disobey = don't obey	unclean = very clean	rewrite = don't write
unwell = well again	retell = don't tell	misbehave = behave wrongly
unable = not able	incomplete = not complete	preview = view before

Puzzle 2:

unhappy = very happy	dislike = don't like	rebuild = build before
invisible = very visible	preheat = heat before	unlucky = not lucky
pretest = test before	unsafe = not safe	mistrust = do trust

33. Add to It!

cheerful	→	good mood
courageous	→	bravery
jewelry	→	gem
youngster	→	not old
talkative	→	speak

addition → join together

government → rule

membership → person in a group

34. Get to the Root of It
Definitions will vary.

1. **act** — behave a certain way
2. **subtract** — take away
3. **expect** — think something will happen
4. **spice** — plant part used to flavor food
5. **doubt** — uncertainty
6. **air** — oxygen that people breathe
7. **behave** — act nicely
8. **usual** — normal
9. **luck** — chance
10. **friend** — someone who likes you and you like back

35. Word + Word
1. **light**house
2. snow**man**
3. foot**ball**
4. **sun**flower
5. butter**fly**
6. table**cloth**
7. **sun**set
8. **foot**print
9. **popcorn**
10. **scarecrow**

36. Word Whiz
1. sun + <u>glasses</u> = <u>sunglasses</u>
2. sand + <u>box</u> = <u>sandbox</u>
3. post + <u>card</u> = <u>postcard</u>
4. hair + <u>cut</u> = <u>haircut</u>
5. fire + <u>place</u> = <u>fireplace</u>
6. cow + <u>boy</u> = <u>cowboy</u>

7. rain + <u>coat</u> = <u>raincoat</u>
8. key + <u>hole</u> = <u>keyhole</u>
9. snow + <u>flake</u> = <u>snowflake</u>
10. base + <u>ball</u> = <u>baseball</u>

37. Good, Great, Awesome!
1. humongous
2. fantastic
3. thunderous
4. gorgeous
5. enormous
6. frosty
7. scorching
8. golden
9. hilarious
10. ancient

38. Burst of Energy
sleep → **snooze**; cry → **whimper**; disappear → **vanish**; throw → **hurl**; bother → **annoy**; ask → **question**; drink → **slurp**; walk → **tiptoe**; hold → **clutch**; break → **shatter**

39. Fact vs. Opinion
1. Fact
2. Opinion
3. Opinion
4. Fact
5. Fact
6. Opinion
7. Fact
8. Opinion
9. Opinion
10. Fact
11. Fact
12. Opinion

40. The Perfect Pet
Answers will vary.

41. Getting Organized
Answers will vary.

42. You're the Expert
Answers will vary.

43. Polar Bear Information
Polar bears have four legs and a whitish coat. → **Description**

Baby polar bears are the size of a stick of butter when they are first born. The babies grow quickly and in a couple of months weigh 20 pounds. → **Sequence**

Polar bears and grizzly bears are both big and powerful. Their coats are different colors. → **Compare and Contrast**

Polar bears live in the icy arctic circle. Climate change is causing arctic ice to melt. Polar bears are losing more and more of their habitat each year. → **Cause and Effect**

Ice is difficult to walk on. Polar bears have grips on the pads of their feet that keep them from slipping. → **Problem and Solution**

44. Imagine That!
Answers will vary.

45. Hooray for Me!
Answers will vary.

Part 3: Math

1. Problem Solver
1. 24 + 48 = 72
2. 60 − 48 = 12
3. 21 + 18 + 19 = 58
4. 77 − 43 + 15 = 49
5. 26 + 68 = 94
6. **100 − (37 + 28)** = 35

2. Math in the Forest
1. 25 + 13 + 52 = 90
2. 69 − 27 = 42
3. 80 − 13 + 27 = 94
4. 47 − 14 = 33
5. 88 − 69 = 19

3. Family Tree

4. Learning to Ride

5. A Pair of Pears
1. yes   9 + 9 = 18
2. yes   8 + 8 = 16
3. no
4. yes   10 + 10 = 20
5. no
6. yes
7. no
8. no

6. Snack Time

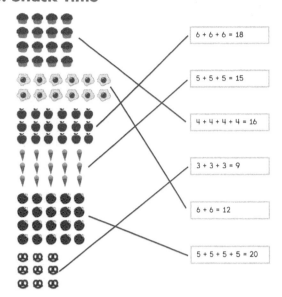

6 + 6 + 6 = 18	
5 + 5 + 5 = 15	
4 + 4 + 4 + 4 = 16	
3 + 3 + 3 = 9	
6 + 6 = 12	
5 + 5 + 5 + 5 = 20	

7. Sports Store

1. 5 + 5 + 5 + 5 = 20 (given)
2. 8 + 8 = 16
3. 4 + 4 + 4 = 12
4. 5 + 5 + 5 = 15
5. 6 + 6 + 6 = 18
6. 4 + 4 + 4 + 4 = 16
7. 5 + 5 + 5 + 5 + 5 = 25
8. 7 + 7 = 14

8. Hundreds, Tens, and Ones

1. 8 hundreds   4 tens   5 ones
2. 9 hundreds   7 tens   8 ones
3. 1 hundred   0 tens   7 ones
4. 2 hundreds   6 tens   7 ones
5. 7 hundreds   4 tens   3 ones
6. 6 hundreds   9 tens   0 ones
7. 5 hundreds   5 tens   5 ones
8. 4 hundreds   0 tens   1 one
9. 2 hundreds   3 tens   4 ones
10. 4 hundreds   3 tens   2 ones
11. 650   **12.** 802   **13.** 331.
         14. 267   **15.** 462

9. Lucky 7

Puzzle 1: Hundreds

799	672	177
237	751	407
771	705	727

Puzzle 2: Hundreds

347	172	729
977	777	207
751	173	478

Puzzle 3: Ones

707	751	622
197	987	706
347	174	567

10. Bundle Up!

1. 2 hundreds   7 tens   4 ones   =   274
2. 1 hundred   4 tens   8 ones   =   148
3. 4 hundreds   3 tens   6 ones   =   436
4. 3 hundreds   2 tens   9 ones   =   329

11. Base Ten Blocks

1. 300   2. 400   3. 100   4. 800
5. 500   6. 300   7. 300   8. 200
9. 300   **10.** 100

12. Hop, Skip, Jump!

1. 25, 50, 75
2. 60, 140, 190
3. 300, 800
4. 920, 945, 980
5. 560, 600, 690

13. Super Speedy

14. Make a Match

Seven hundred ninety-nine → **799**

Three hundred forty-two → **342**

Six hundred forty-five → **645**

Four hundred three → **403**

Nine hundred twenty-four → **924**

Five hundred sixty-one → **561**

Eight hundred fourteen → **814**

One hundred thirty-six → **136**

Two hundred twenty-two → **222**

Eight hundred → **800**

15. More than One Way

1. 70 + 14 + 4
2. eight hundred thirty-six
3. four hundred five
4. 300 + 50 + 7
5. 207
6. 591
7. 725
8. 346
9. 891
10. 478
11. 900 + 90 + 9
12. 500 + 60 + 5
13. 300 + 70 + 1
14. 600 + 40 + 2
15. 100 + 80 + 3

16. Alligator Bites

795 < 899   245 < 254

863 = 863   377 < 773

552 < 553   408 < 480

458 > 452   702 > 699

603 = 603   400 < 500

999 > 599   300 < 301

197 < 200   507 > 500

309 < 390   169 < 691

212 > 121   888 = 888

303 > 283   990 > 909

17. Break It Up

23 + 48 = ?

<u>20</u> + <u>3</u> + <u>40</u> + <u>8</u>
tens   ones   tens   ones

Add the tens: <u>20</u> + <u>40</u> = <u>60</u>

Add the ones: <u>3</u> + <u>8</u> = <u>11</u>

How many in all? <u>60</u> + <u>11</u> = <u>71</u>

Now we know that: 23 + 48 = <u>71</u>

36 + 36 = ?

<u>30</u> + <u>6</u> + <u>30</u> + <u>6</u>
tens   ones   tens   ones

Add the tens: <u>30</u> + <u>30</u> = <u>60</u>

Add the ones: <u>6</u> + <u>6</u> = <u>12</u>

How many in all? <u>60</u> + <u>12</u> = <u>72</u>

Now we know that: 36 + 36 = <u>72</u>

48 + 19 = ?

<u>40</u> + <u>8</u> + <u>10</u> + <u>9</u>
tens   ones   tens   ones

Add the tens: <u>40</u> + <u>10</u> = <u>50</u>

Add the ones: <u>8</u> + <u>9</u> = <u>17</u>

How many in all? <u>50</u> + <u>17</u> = <u>67</u>

Now we know that: 48 + 19 = <u>67</u>

18. Good Neighbors

1

```
  1
 5 7
+2 5
─────
 8 2
```

5

```
 6 1
-4 2
─────
 1 9
```

1

```
 1 9
+4 2
─────
 6 1
```

6

```
 7 4
-3 6
─────
 3 8
```

1

```
 5 5
+3 8
─────
 9 3
```

7

```
 8 2
-2 5
─────
 5 7
```

```
 4 6
+3 2
─────
 7 8
```

```
 9 9
-5 5
─────
 4 4
```

1

```
 3 8
+1 6
─────
 5 4
```

8

```
 9 3
-3 8
─────
 5 5
```

1

```
 3 6
+3 8
─────
 7 4
```

4

```
 5 4
-1 6
─────
 3 8
```

```
 4 4
+5 5
─────
 9 9
```

```
 7 8
-3 2
─────
 4 6
```

5

```
 5 7
+4 0
─────
 9 7
```

```
 6 8
-1 9
─────
 4 9
```

19. Sporty Shopping Spree

46 + 15 + 37 + 25 = $123

35 + 37 + 23 + 18 = $113

32 + 37 + 9 + 23 = $101

66 + 37 + 23 + 25 = $151

20. It All Adds Up!

23 + 38 + 14 + 18 → (20 + 3) +
                       (30 + 8) +
                       (10 + 4) +
                       (10 + 8)

```
 36 →      (30 + 10 + 20) +
 12        (6 + 2 + 9 + 4)
 29
+ 4
────
```

29 + 42 + 16 + 31 → 29
                          42
                          16
                       + 31

(10 + 60 + 30 + 10) + (7 + 5 + 6)
→ 128

116 → (40 + 20 + 10 + 30) +
       (5 + 9 + 2)

(40 + 5) + (10 + 6) + (20 + 8) +
(30 + 6) → 45 + 16 + 28 + 36

21. Math Super Star

1 1

```
 3 4 7
+2 8 5
───────
 6 3 2
```

5

```
 8 6 1
-7 4 2
───────
 1 1 9
```

```
 4 0 3
+2 7 9
───────
 6 8 2
```

```
 9 4 5
-7 4 2
───────
 2 0 3
```

```
 5 0 6
+3 9 1
───────
 8 9 7
```

```
 2 7 9
-1 2 2
───────
 1 5 7
```

```
  1 1            7
  2 9 9        6 8 3
+ 1 0 5      − 2 4 5
─────        ─────
  4 0 4        4 3 8

  1            6
  6 0 4        7 1 8
+ 3 6 6      − 1 4 3
─────        ─────
  9 7 0        5 7 5

  1            8
  6 4 3        9 1 2
+ 2 0 8      − 1 5 2
─────        ─────
  8 5 1        7 6 0
```

22. Which Tool to Choose?

12-inch ruler: sneaker, pencil, book

Meter stick: tomato plant, cat, quilt

Measuring tape: person's head, soccer ball, person's waist

23. How Much Longer?

1. How long is the pencil?
   <u>18</u> centimeters
   How long is the crayon? <u>9</u> centimeters
   How much longer is the pencil?
   <u>9 centimeters</u>

2. How long is the paper clip?
   <u>2</u> inches
   How long is the marker? <u>6</u> inches
   How much longer is the marker?
   <u>4 inches</u>

3. How long is the eraser? <u>6</u> inches
   How long is the chalk? <u>3</u> inches
   What is the difference in length between the two objects? <u>3 inches</u>

24. At the Fair

1. 6 inches
2. 4 inches
3. 15 feet
4. 3 feet

5. 33 centimeters
6. 2 feet
7. 57 feet
8. 8 centimeters

25. Ready, Set, Measure!

1–10 Answers will vary.

11. <

12. >

26. How to Measure a Whale

1. inches
2. feet
3. meters
4. centimeters
5. inches
6. inches
7. centimeters
8. feet
9. feet
10. meters

27. Best Guess

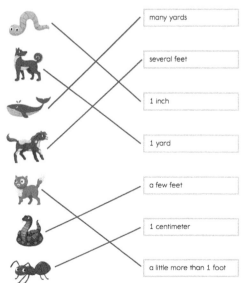

28. Spring Planting

1. $20 + 15 + 20 + 15 = 70$ feet
2. $84 - 48 = 36$ inches
3. $29 + 29 + 29 = 87$ inches
4. $72 - 48 = 24$ inches
5. $18 + 15 + 19 = 52$ feet
6. $24 + 9 = 33$ inches

29. Measuring the Animal Kingdom

1. The gorilla grew 17 inches.
   $53 - 36 = 17$
2. The humpback whale is 24 feet longer than a killer whale.
   $49 - 25 = 24$
3. The mother giraffe is 12 feet taller than her baby.
   $19 - 7 = 12$
4. The kangaroo jumped 68 feet.
   $23 + 21 + 24 = 68$
5. The cheetah ran 3 fewer meters.
   $81 - 78 = 3$
6. The adult elephant's tusk is 48 inches longer than the baby's.
   $72 - 24 = 48$
7. The worm crawled 84 inches.
   $26 + 36 + 22 = 84$

30. Playground Fun

1. $11 + 6 = 17$ feet
2. $13 + 8 = 21$ feet
3. $8 - 3 = 5$ feet
4. $15 + 3 = 18$ yards

31. Carpenter Caper

1. $84 - 54 = 30$ inches
2. $49 + 28 = 77$ inches
3. $10 + 9 = 19$ feet
4. $21 - 5 = 16$ feet
5. $7 + 7 = 14$ centimeters

32. Tick Tock, Tick Tock

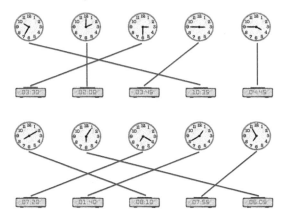

33. Lucy's Busy Day

1. Lucy woke up at 7:45 a.m.
2. What time did Lucy have breakfast? __8:30 a.m.__
3. Lucy had a picnic lunch with Bear at 12:15 p.m.
4. What time did Lucy play soccer? __3:30 p.m.__
5. Lucy took a bath after dinner at 7:00 p.m.
6. What time did Lucy fall asleep? __8:20 p.m.__

34. Piggy Bank Savings

35. Beach Shop

1. $2.72   YES
2. $3.29   NO
3. $3.36   YES
4. $3.11   YES

36. How Does Your Garden Grow?

Tomato Plants:

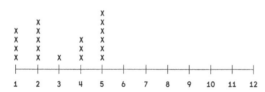

Pepper Plants:

Sunflower Plants:

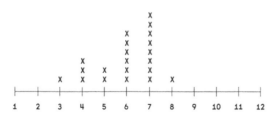

37. Getting Good at Graphing

1. basketball
2. football
3. 9
4. 5
5. 7
6. 2
7. same
8. 4
9. 20

38. Getting in Shape

Number of Edges	Number of Angles	Real-Life Example
0	0	Answers will vary.
3	3	Answers will vary.
	4	Answers will vary.
4	4	Answers will vary.
4	4	Answers will vary.
5	5	Answers will vary.
6	6	Answers will vary.

39. Quadrilateral Quiz

Puzzle 1:

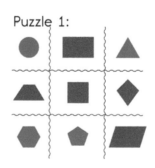

Puzzle 2:

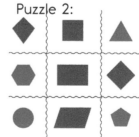

40. The Shape of Things

 cube

 cone

 sphere

 circle

 hexagon

 square

 cone

 diamond

 rectangle

 cube

pentagon

triangle

41. Quilting Bee

1.

2.

3. How many rows? **4**
   How many columns? **3**
   How many square patches does the quilt have? **12**

4. How many patches does this quilt have? **24**

42. Community Garden

1. How many equal shares? **16**

2. How many equal shares? **8**

3. How many equal shares? **15**

4. How many equal shares? **6**

5. How many equal shares? **6**

6. How many equal shares? **9**

43. Fair Share

Answers will vary. Possible answers:

4 equal parts

Fourths

Halves

Halves

2 equal parts

Thirds

6 equal parts

3 equal parts

Halves

44. Even Steven

Answers will vary.

1. Possible answers:

2. Possible answers:

3. Possible answers:

4. Possible answers:

5. Possible answers:

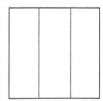

45. Dividing Line

1.

2.

3.

4.

5.

6.

7.

8.

9.

10.

About the Author

Martha Day Zschock is a former elementary school teacher and a bestselling children's book author and illustrator. Her first book, *Journey Around Cape Cod and the Islands from A to Z*, has grown into a series that includes 10 different locations. She also writes the Hello! series of board books. Follow her latest journeys at MarthaZschock.com.

Printed in the USA
CPSIA information can be obtained
at www.ICGtesting.com
LVHW060549060724
784545LV00005B/12